4 $\frac{5|15}{11|15}$

3 $\frac{12|11}{10|12}$

THE FOREVER PORTFOLIO

THE FOREVER

*How to Pick Stocks That You Can Hold
for the Long Run*

PORTFOLIO

JAMES ALTUCHER

Portfolio

PORTFOLIO
Published by the Penguin Group
Penguin Group (USA) Inc., 375 Hudson Street, New York, New York 10014, U.S.A.
Penguin Group (Canada), 90 Eglinton Avenue East, Suite 700, Toronto, Ontario, Canada M4P 2Y3
(a division of Pearson Penguin Canada Inc.)
Penguin Books Ltd, 80 Strand, London WC2R 0RL, England
Penguin Ireland, 25 St. Stephen's Green, Dublin 2, Ireland (a division of Penguin Books Ltd)
Penguin Books Australia Ltd, 250 Camberwell Road, Camberwell, Victoria 3124, Australia
(a division of Pearson Australia Group Pty Ltd)
Penguin Books India Pvt Ltd, 11 Community Centre, Panchsheel Park, New Delhi – 110 017, India
Penguin Group (NZ), 67 Apollo Drive, Rosedale, North Shore 0632, New Zealand
(a division of Pearson New Zealand Ltd)
Penguin Books (South Africa) (Pty) Ltd, 24 Sturdee Avenue, Rosebank,
Johannesburg 2196, South Africa

Penguin Books Ltd, Registered Offices: 80 Strand, London WC2R 0RL, England

First published in 2008 by Portfolio, a member of Penguin Group (USA) Inc.

1   3   5   7   9   10   8   6   4   2

Copyright © James Altucher, 2008
All rights reserved

PUBLISHER'S NOTE: This publication is designed to provide accurate and authoritative information in regard to the subject matter covered. It is sold with the understanding that the publisher is not engaged in rendering legal, accounting or other professional services. If you require legal advice or other expert assistance, you should seek the services of a competent professional.

Materials from Yahoo!: Reproduced with permission of Yahoo! Inc. © 2008 by Yahoo! Inc. Yahoo! and the Yahoo! logo are trademarks of Yahoo! Inc.

Charts on pages 138 and 139: © 2008 Morningstar, Inc. All rights reserved. The information contained herein: (1) is proprietary to Morningstar and/or its content providers; (2) may not be copied or distributed; and (3) is not warranted to be accurate, complete, or timely. Neither Morningstar nor its content providers are responsible for any dangers or losses arising from any use of this information. Past performance is no guarantee of future results.

LIBRARY OF CONGRESS CATALOGING IN PUBLICATION DATA
Altucher, James.
The forever portfolio : how to pick stocks that you can hold for the long run / James Altucher.
p.   cm.
Includes bibliographical references and index.
ISBN 978-1-59184-211-8
1. Investments.   2. Stocks.   3. Portfolio management.   I. Title.
HG4521.A45587 2008
332.63'22—dc22   2008018197

Printed in the United States of America
Designed by Chris Welch

To Josie and Mollie

FOREWORD

If you are anything like me, you will love how James Altucher thinks, you will love what he has to say, you will love the tone of his writing, and you will end up loving James Altucher himself.

But that alone would not be a reason to read his book. There are a lot of lovable people in the world. (Well, maybe not as many as there used to be, but still . . .) There are also a lot of very smart people, particularly in the world of finance, and James is certainly among them. What strikes me as most noteworthy about James is that he combines a high level of intellectual firepower with an even higher level of common sense. He is a good thinker in part because he refuses to overthink. Also, his brain seems configured to generate the kind of insights that seem obvious in retrospect but which none of the other geniuses manage to notice. Do you know the story about the economist and the $20 bill? It goes like this: An economist is walking down the street with a friend, and the friend spots what looks like a $20 bill lying on the sidewalk. The economist, knowing what he knows about market efficiencies, blithely disabuses his friend: "It can't be a $20 bill. If it were, somebody else would have already picked it up."

James Altucher, meanwhile, would have just picked up the $20 and gone on his way, a bit richer and a bit happier. Or, as he writes in *The Forever Portfolio,* "You don't need to know advanced physics to see the color of a rainbow." James finds the silver lining in all sorts of clouds but, just as important, he also seems to know when a sunny sky is about to cloud over.

This book is putatively about global demographic trends over the next fifty years and how to wisely invest in them. Indeed, it does cover that ground. But it does more. It encourages you to think creatively, wisely, and sanely about investing, an arena in which creativity, wisdom, and sanity are often in short supply. James is especially good at making silk purses from sows' ears. He finds the upside in identity theft, obesity, bot armies, and traffic fatalities. Some may grumble that he is ghoulish, preying on American vices and weakness in order to profit. That is a moral argument best addressed in a different sort of book than this one. What I will say about James personally is that he is a good and kind man, humane, a mensch even.

This does not mean he is without his flaws. Hardly. Fortunately, this also makes for good reading. Although this book is full of actual facts and reality-based information, it is the personal writing, peppered in amid the rest, that is my favorite. His gambling stories are particularly good, but so are his stories about how to generate useful ideas.

I met James several years ago while writing a book about the psychology of money. He was easily the most captivating character I had run across. (Sadly, that book got put in a drawer; reading *The Forever Portfolio* made me want to pull it out again.) James was just coming out of a funk, having made a great deal of money and then, in a spectacular sort of psychological hara-kiri, losing most of it. We first started talking in the huge Tribeca loft he had bought for his family and which he'd soon be forced to sell. The building had once housed a sailcloth factory. Although the Altuchers had done a state-of-the-art renovation, the place was still so cavernous that you could well imagine it a century earlier, teeming with a sweaty crew of Portuguese or Italians as they wrestled bolts of canvas onto the cutting frames. How quaint it now seemed: the idea that riches were once made in the manufacture of something as prosaic as ships' sails. The Altuchers' wondrous apartment stood as a capitalist testament to how many means there are to fortune-making, and how quickly those means can change.

The Forever Portfolio represents everything that James Altucher learned from his own reversal of fortune, and everything he has learned since. There is almost nothing in this book that isn't thought provoking. I hope you read it with the same pleasure that I did.

—Stephen J. Dubner,
coauthor of *Freakonomics*

CONTENTS

THE FOREVER PORTFOLIO

I don't like to worry. This seems like an obvious statement, hardly worth mentioning in the first lines of a substantial investing book. But the reality is, most people do like to worry. They worry about their investments on a day-to-day basis. They worry about their weight, even though minute by minute there's almost nothing they can do to change it. They worry about what their boss thinks of them, or they overanalyze the latest e-mails from colleagues, superiors, boyfriends, or girlfriends. People stay up late at night worrying, or they wake up in the middle of the night, plagued by whatever is on their minds.

The human brain has an urge to be active, and in the absence of anything important, the mind creates things to fill the space. These thoughts cover the spectrum, from fretting about a possible terrorist attack to worrying about money, retirement, the health of one's parents, and so on. And these thoughts could easily be those of a twenty-seven-year-old.

I'll give you a specific example. In 1999, I was buying an apartment. It was during the height of the tech boom, and I was flush with illiquid paper trading at fairly lofty values. I thought I was rich. I found a beautiful 4,500-square-foot loft with roof access. The real-estate broker showed me a few more places, but I was hooked on that initial apartment. As a last "check the box" moment I asked my broker, Nancy, one final thing: What happens if terrorists blow up the building next door?

"You can't live your life that way," Nancy, being the good saleswoman she was, replied. And she was right. Life is short, and the only way we can enjoy it and the relatively few moments we are all given is to not spend them anxious and nervous, constructing fictional scenarios that can drive us crazy. Unfortunately, as it turned out, terrorists did blow up the building next door: The apartment I bought was right next to the World Trade Center. Nothing could alleviate the tragedy that engulfed the families of the victims of the attacks, and the entire neighborhood was completely submerged in the aftermath. Everyone was affected. Lives were lost, the financial markets plunged, and businesses and investment capital were put on hold for years.

The scars of that day of infamy are so deep, it is fair to say that the nation never really recovered. But the great thing about a global economy is that it does recuperate as opportunity finds its way back into the financial system. The key to investing, then, is staying in the game, consistently looking for opportunity and not worrying about all of those things that are meaningless or out of your control.

Why start a book on investing with this discussion of worry? Because this book is not about how to get rich or how to achieve 100 percent returns or whatever it is that most investment books are about. This book is about how to eliminate the distractions so that you can make sound investment decisions, rest easy, and enjoy all of the other aspects of your life. You don't want to have to look at your investments every day for the rest of your life. You don't want to have to follow every tick of the markets or panic if they plunge 10 percent in a week, as they often do.

You want to make long-term bets that will pay off handsomely over the long run because of overwhelming demographic trends and other factors that will be explained in this book. You want to cash in on the trends that will overtake the investment world like a tidal wave. Remember, tidal waves are there for us to surf on top of, not be drowned by.

The style of thinking described in this book does not apply only to your investment decisions; it is also applicable to all areas of your business life, from deciding on entrepreneurial ventures (which is, of course, a form of investment) to career decisions and whatever it is you do every day.

Let's look at the investment world for a second. Money is a scarce resource. Many people want it, and there's only so much money to go around. You have to think of it this way: There's a lot of competition for the dollars you want to put in your pocket. In the investment world, you have some very smart people vying to screw you out of that money. Consider the following examples:

COMPETITION FOR YOUR DOLLARS

Warren Buffett. I am being slightly facetious here. Warren Buffett clearly doesn't want to pick your pocket. Or does he? He's the smartest investor ever, and as I write this, he's sitting on a stash of $75 billion. Buffett, because this is the sort of thing he's done for the past fifty years, would like to turn that $75 billion into $100 billion over the next few years. That's $25 billion he needs to get that nobody else can put their hands on. If it's a choice between him and you, he chooses himself. And when I say "Warren Buffett" here, I mean every superinvestor out there, from Carl Icahn to George Soros to T. Boone Pickens and many others of the elite who have superior skill in analyzing demographics, fundamentals, and trends and sizing up their competition so they can consistently, year in and year out, hone their talent of wealth accumulation. Let me just say flat-out, you can't compete with these people. They are better than you and me. It's important that you acknowledge that right up front. You never want to get into a ring with an investor of this ilk.

Later on we'll learn how to piggyback on the best investors out there. Meanwhile, here's a brief list of some of the competitors that are fighting for your hard-earned dollars in the financial markets:

- Hedge funds
- Mutual funds
- Day traders

Hedge funds. These are unregulated investment pools that currently manage more than $2 trillion in assets. The people managing hedge funds use sophisticated analytic tools to identify and take advantage of undervalued investments. Why would an investment be underpriced? Well, for one thing, people are, on the whole, not very smart. In other words, they worry too much, and that worry crowds out the otherwise intelligent thoughts that would've been allowed to flourish if not pushed aside. I'll give you an extreme example: In 2002, because of the dot-com bust, many public Internet companies that raised a ton of cash during the boom were trading for less than the cash they had in the bank. People were worried that the Internet was nothing more than a scam, simply because a batch of IPOs in late 1999 and early 2000 went public without any revenues or earnings and ended up costing investors a lot of money. Fair enough, but the Internet population was still growing at over 100 percent per year even during the stock market bust. E-commerce was growing, and even online advertising was starting to pick up. The Internet couldn't care less about the stock market. It was a tidal wave.

But that didn't stop investors from selling shares in every e-, .com, and i- company they could find. For example, ValueClick (VCLK) had $80 million cash in the bank, profits, and an entire market cap of $50 million. In other words, you could buy the whole company for $50 million and then put your hands on the $80 million in the bank. It didn't make sense. Hedge funds went in, scooped up shares, and made a ton of money.

I've traded for hedge funds, and I've invested in hedge funds. These people will kill you when they see you. They hate you. They will scar you for life and laugh while they do it.

But we don't need to compete against them. A couple of years ago, I was recording a video at TheStreet.com with Jim Cramer. This was early in his reign as financial TV's champion as the host of the CNBC show *Mad Money*. I asked him how the average investor can hope to compete against hedge funds, and he had a great response. "Hedge funds," Cramer said, "are slaves to the monthly number. They have to report consistent and upbeat numbers, or their investors will bail on them. Retail investors don't have to report monthly numbers and so can take advantage of this structural flaw in how hedge funds are set up." He knows this all too well, and I highly recommend reading the chapter in his book *Confessions of a Street Addict* on the pain he went through in September 1998, when he faced mass redemptions from even his most loyal investors.

COMMENTARY VERSUS NEWS

I've been writing for TheStreet.com since 2002. It was started in 1996 by successful hedge-fund manager Jim Cramer with the idea that it would be a twist on the traditional financial media. Most financial media (e.g., The *Wall Street Journal*) are news organizations. News happens (the Fed cuts rates, Wal-Mart reports earnings, Apple releases a new product) and the typical financial media organization will attempt to report that news without any bias.

For good reasons, reporters have been discouraged from having investments and showing any bias in their reporting. It's too easy to manipulate stocks with news reporting. You report something good (even if it's inaccurate) about a stock, and the stock will go up 5 percent in minutes. There have been several cases in which reporters or public-relations firms have done this inappropriately and even illegally.

However, Jim's twist was to say, "Get the best money managers to write about stocks, disclose everything, and then say what you really think about a situation," the idea being that if a professional money manager owns Wal-Mart, then he is probably a better resource for investors who want to understand Wal-Mart's earnings. When you're in the trenches with a stock, you're going to put a lot more mental energy into understanding what's going on with that stock and its earnings or news events. And, as a business, a financial media organization that does this is going to have a lot more people paying attention to it. People want to make money, they don't want to just read the news. They are hungry for ideas. The typical financial media organization won't give them those ideas. When I later started Stockpickr.com, the idea was to take it one step further—no news at all, just raw stock ideas plus the portfolios of all the best investors out there.

I cover later how I met Jim and started writing for TheStreet.com, but suffice it to say that I knew the company for many years. I started a company in the nineties that built Web sites for media companies. One of these was a tiny operation called TheStreet.com, and for that job I had to do a study of all the news sites out there. It was then that I started to note the subtle differences between TheStreet.com and, say, CNN.com.

Jim took the whole genre one step further when he started his *Mad Money* show. As an aside, when he began dress rehearsals for the show, about a month before it first aired, he asked me to go on. He wanted to try out the idea of having guests. At the time, I was really bullish on two third-tier search-engine companies, Terra Lycos and Ask Jeeves. Both had a ton of cash and were barely trading above cash levels, so I felt that they could get bought. Jim never likes bad companies, so in the search-engine space he liked Google. We argued on our segment about first-tier versus third-tier companies. Within the next three months both Terra Lycos and Ask Jeeves got acquired about 20–30 percent higher than where they were that day—and Google went on to move up 200 percent higher. Still, I did horribly on TV. I just can't seem to get the hang of it. Consequently, I was never a guest on *Mad Money* again.

I have my own experience with this. Having run a fund of hedge funds, I've been on the opposite side of this equation. A fund of hedge funds invests in other hedge funds rather than directly in stocks or other investments. A fund of hedge funds wants to balance its investments so that in every market condition, it still offers positive returns every month. When a hedge fund I invested in had a down month, I really wanted to know why. If the reasons weren't good, I would start thinking about redeeming my investment. For better or worse, that was how the game was played.

Anytime there's a structural disadvantage like this, it creates a crack in the space-time continuum that makes up the global economy. In that crack grow the seeds of opportunity in which money can be made.

Mutual funds. With twenty thousand mutual funds, which have more than $10 trillion in assets, there is no doubt that this is a fearsome competitor for our dollars. The reality is, however, that those mutual funds have their own structural disadvantages. The people who manage them are afraid to underperform each other. So they all hug a benchmark (for instance, the returns of the S&P 500) and they tend to just buy the large-cap members of these indices so that their returns closely mimic the returns of that benchmark. It's important for an investor in a mutual fund to know that a mutual fund is not considered a success if it does well; it's only considered a success if it does well relative to its peers. For example, if a mutual fund is an "energy fund" (meaning it focuses on stocks in the energy sector), then the fund is considered successful if it does much better than the universe of energy stocks. So if energy stocks in general are up 20 percent for the year and the mutual fund is only up 15 percent, then that's considered a failure. This is called "relative performance" as opposed to "absolute performance." Absolute performance just asks the question "Was the fund up or down?" If up, then good. If down, then bad. A mutual fund is considered a truly great fund not if it is up every year but if it outperforms its peers and its benchmark every year.

Day traders. When I think of the term *day trader*, I think back to 1999 when people were waking up in the morning, getting a hundred shares of the latest IPO and selling them two hundred points higher after the company opened up. That game, believe it or not, created many hundred-millionaires. People had this game that was called "playing the calendar": Let's say investment bank XYZ was bringing out a hot dot-com company in an IPO. Two to four weeks before the IPO, the guys who played the calendar would suddenly start trading back and forth hundreds of thousands of shares of random companies, and using XYZ as the broker and thus generating millions of dollars in commissions for XYZ. Sometimes the traders would lose on this; sometimes they would break even. It didn't matter. What mattered was that when the IPO came out, they would place an order for shares at the IPO price and then sell those shares within minutes of the stock trading up to 200 points higher on an unsuspecting retail audience that was eager to scoop up the latest hot Internet company. That game completely dried up in 2000, but it lasted long enough to create untold riches for those who took advantage of it. I visited a guy a few years ago who was one of the biggest calendar players. He started from scratch in the midnineties, and this was the only strategy he played. He's retired now, and his art collection alone is worth $300 million.

But when that game changed, so did the nature of day trading. I started day trading in 2002 and continued through 2004, ultimately trading for several hedge funds. The entire game for me was to take advantage of very short-term volatility on the short or the long side, which I described in an earlier book, *Trade Like a Hedge Fund*. I would model the markets using software I built on top of the software package Wealth-Lab (now owned by Fidelity). As a simple example, let's say the S&P 500 was down four days in a row and the fourth day was the last day of the month. I would look at the last thirty times this had happened and see if any events had a high likelihood of happening on the fifth day. For instance, maybe in twenty-nine out of thirty times, the Nasdaq went up five points on the first hour of the fifth day. I would then make that trade accordingly.

Believe me, there were days this was the best job on the planet. I would wake up, look at all the stats, make my trade at the open, and fifteen minutes later be out of the trade with a nice profit and be done for the day. What would I do then? My biggest regret is that I didn't watch more movies or take more walks by the river. I would usually find things to worry about that years later I can now look back on and say were of no consequence whatsoever. I really wish I had taken advantage of the positive aspects of day trading, because there were certainly other days on which this was the *worst* job imaginable.

On days like those, all I would need were five Nasdaq points to hit my goal and the market would crawl its way upwards to three, three and a half, four points, maybe even reaching five without quite hitting my sell order, and then immediately drop down and slowly bleed me for the rest of the day. I would be stupidly glued to the screen, watching every tick. It was incredibly painful and such a waste of time and mental energy. I hated it. With every downtick in the market, I would feel my blood pulsing all over my body. Needless to say, this was not fun.

Furthermore, day traders are not your competitors. They are thrashing about right now, looking for the latest momentum idea that's going to pop that day. In the long run, the only people making money from the day-trading business are the brokers. The brokers who cater to this community tend to do very well as long as they keep their costs and risk management in check during the inevitable cycles.

A fundamental flaw the day traders have is the belief that not holding stocks overnight is somehow safe. If you hold stocks overnight, they argue, what happens when nuclear war breaks out while you are asleep? You'll wake up and your stocks will be worthless. My feeling is the same as my real-estate agent's: you can't live your life that way. For one thing, we have more serious problems than stock values if there's a nuclear war. In addition, let's just look at history. Since 1992, the beginning of the nineties bull market (arguably the greatest bull market of any market in history in terms of dollar size, returns, and lasting effect), what would have happened if you had only held stocks overnight? The reality is, since 1997, just buying the close on the S&P 500 each night and selling first thing in the morning (i.e. only holding stocks overnight) you would've returned 110 percent instead of the 34 percent that the S&P 500 returns. In other words, all of the gains on the S&P 500 (and then some) occurred overnight in the past ten years. Just holding during the day would've lost money. The reality is, the best way to make money in the stock market is to buy for the long haul and ignore the day trade—like blips and anxieties that constantly seize the markets. The market truly is like a soap opera. But most soap operas are pretty boring, besides being poorly written and acted. Better to take it slow and remove yourself from the drama.

Mutual-fund managers, hedge-fund managers, day traders, and every professional in the investment sector would grab your wallet if they saw you in a dark alley. They don't like you, and they all think they are smarter than you. Maybe they're right. But like the great warrior of Greek mythology, Achilles, they all have their weak spots, and taking advantage of those Achilles' heels can make us money. Not only that, but being able to identify these weaknesses can help us whether our goal is to make good stock investments, start businesses, enhance our career choices, or identify new projects to develop.

Overall, the most important factor is to identify the trends over the next several decades that we can ride to investment success—trends that will allow us to rest easy, knowing they are in full force no matter what enemies are trying to block our path. Being able to sleep soundly is an important factor in making money, and the only way you can do so is if you don't fight the forces that challenge us all every day. In the chapters that follow, we will be looking at investment, career, and even entrepreneurial choices from several angles. This book will focus on getting correct answers to the following two questions:

1. **What are the tidal wave–like demographic forces taking shape around the world that we can surf on top of?** These trends include the ever-increasing need for clean water, the worldwide rise in obesity, the need for better health care for retiring Baby Boomers, the need for improved methods for removing tattoos (yes, this is a trend), and many more.
2. **What are the methods for identifying opportunities and companies in each demographic trend that we focus on?** The primary method is looking at companies with financially secure balance sheets and strong, extremely successful investors already invested in them. There's no guarantee that these investors will stay invested forever, but it's a guarantee that they did the homework and research required to make an investment decision, and that's a good starting point for us.

Throughout the book I will be singling out stocks for inclusion in a "forever portfolio." I do not intend for every one of these stocks to go up every month or even every year. But over time, the goal is to invest in stocks that will still be here fifty years from now, and that's possible by simply following the two methods above. Find the stocks that overlap broad demographic trends, with strong investment professionals already behind them.

Also, not every chapter in this book is about stocks or investing.

No one financial strategy is an island. One of the other goals of this book is to develop a "forever approach" to career, entrepreneurial-ism, and your overall life outlook. Those are the secondary themes of the book. The primary goal is to help you to develop your own forever portfolio, using the demographic and other methods that will be covered throughout.

┌─────┐
│ **1** │
└─────┘

Don't Be a Forever Contrarian

My favorite word as a kid was *antidisestablishmentarian-ism*, which, at twenty-eight letters, I believed was the longest word in the English language. At the time, I thought it referred to some biology thing, like a disease. It actually means, however, "the people against the people against the government" and originally referred to those opposing the separation of church and state in nineteenth-century England.

I have to coin a new longest word now, which actually refers to me: *antidisestablishmentcontrarianism*. Don't try to disassemble the meaning through the prefixes and suffixes: I'll just tell you what it means, because I invented it. It means the people against the people against the markets. In other words, I hate people who consider themselves contrarian investors.

Think about it. You hate them, too. They're on TV, in the newspapers, and on financial Web sites. Some call you up with their smug advice. "I make my money going against the crowds," they crow, as if they are above the mindless hordes, the narrow-focused Cyclopes

13

running amok in mad mobs all over Wall Street. In order to be a contrarian investor, you must assume people are stupid. You also have to assume that the masses lose money overall. Furthermore, you have to assume that somehow you have the ability to rise up above this general state of ignorance and be a shining beacon of knowledge and intelligence, someone who knows more than everyone else.

Yes, contrarian investor, I hate you. If you wanted to have a cup of coffee with me I'd instantly turn you down. Who wants to spend time with someone who believes everyone else is stupid?

The thing about contrarian investors, though, is that they're insecure. They constantly need to point out that they are contrarian; they want the masses to recognize their superior status; like high priests throughout history, they need to be acknowledged and worshipped.

But the reality is, the masses are usually right. Let's say, for instance, you were a contrarian on Internet stocks. Well, the masses were buying Internet stocks in 1995. If you were a contrarian then, you would've been wiped out five times over, or more, every time you dove in. Heck, even if you were a contrarian in January 2000, you probably would've been wiped out by February, when most Internet highfliers had their last surge. "No big deal," contrarian pundits reply. "I was a little early then, just like I am now."

And here's how contrarians continue: Americans are leveraged to the hilt; 80 percent of Americans have given up their potential for a rainy day; Americans are going to lose their homes and cars, and their credit cards will get canceled when they can't pay. Retailers will suffer first, because everyone who has been borrowing against their future will stop buying goods. The contrarians say America is on a great downswing that will last over the next century, as inflation skyrockets and tens of millions of jobs are lost.

Yet while the death knell for America has been predicted many times over, the investment graveyards are scattered with the remains of the brave contrarians who have bet against the U.S. economy ever since the Great Depression. (Quick: What's the best market year ever? In 1933, in the middle of the Depression, with 20 percent unemployment, the market rose 100 percent.) When inflation and interest rates were skyrocketing in the early eighties and everyone was stuffing silver into their mattresses, the U.S. markets were on the way to a stunning 1,000 percent gain over the next two decades.

So please ignore the self-proclaimed Cassandras and join the clan of antidisestablishmentcontrarianism.

Instead of finding the trends to bet *against*, look at the trends in this book that you know you can bet *on*, and follow them without worrying about the backlash of volatility that occasionally confronts the contrarians. Throughout this book, we will be looking at companies that take advantage of the trends, the demographic tidal waves over the next fifty years: the rising trend in obesity, the ever increasing need for computer security, the tendency for people worldwide to gamble more each year than the year before, to name a few. In addition to finding these trends, we also try to find the companies that are best positioned to take advantage of these trends; not only because of their secure financial position, their intellectual property, and their competitive stance within their industries, but also because they have the current backing of extremely successful investors. We will show you how to piggyback on proven investors who have already done their homework and placed heavy bets on various stocks.

OK, my rant is over. But in the course of writing this chapter, I researched, for your benefit, the longest word in the English language. It is in fact some biology thing: *pneumonoultramicroscopicsilicovolcanoconiosis*. It's forty-five letters. Knock yourself out.

LONGEST WORDS IN ENGLISH

pneumonoultramicroscopicsilicovolcanoconiosis, also spelled **pneumonoultra-microscopicsilicovolcanokoniosis** (45 letters)

a lung disease caused by breathing in particles of siliceous volcanic dust. This is the longest word in any English dictionary. However, it was coined by Everett Smith, the president of The National Puzzlers' League, in 1935 purely for the purpose of inventing a new "longest word." The *Oxford English Dictionary* describes the word as factitious. Nevertheless it also appears in the *Webster's, Random House,* and *Chambers* dictionaries.

hepaticocholangiocholecystenterostomy (37 letters)

a surgical creation of a connection between the gallbladder and a hepatic duct and between the intestine and the gallbladder. This is the longest word in *Gould's Medical Dictionary.*

supercalifragilisticexpialidocious (34 letters)

made-up adjective used as song title from the Walt Disney movie Mary Poppins. It is in the *Oxford English Dictionary.*

hippopotomonstrosesquipedalian (30 letters)

pertaining to a very long word. From *Mrs. Byrne's Dictionary of Unusual, Obscure, and Preposterous Words.*

floccinaucinihilipilification (29 letters)

an estimation of something as worthless. This is the longest word in the first edition of the *Oxford English Dictionary.* It is interesting that the most common letter in English, *e,* does not appear in this word at all, while *i* occurs a total of nine times. The word dates back to 1741. The *1992 Guinness Book of World Records* calls *floccinaucinihilipilification* the longest real word in the *Oxford English Dictionary,* and refers to *pneumonoultramicroscopicsilicovolcanokoniosis* as the longest made-up one.

antidisestablishmentarianism (28 letters)

the belief that opposes removing the tie between church and state. This is probably the most popular of the "longest words" in recent decades.

honorificabilitudinitatibus (27 letters)

honorableness. The word first appeared in English in 1599, and in 1721 was listed by *Bailey's Dictionary* as the longest word in English. It was used by Shakespeare in *Love's Labour's Lost* (Costard; Act V, Scene I):

> *O, they have lived long on the alms-basket of words.*
> *I marvel thy master hath not eaten thee for a word;*
> *for thou art not so long by the head as*
> *honorificabilitudinitatibus: thou art easier*
> *swallowed than a flap-dragon.*

Shakespeare does not use any other words more than 17 letters in length.

electroencephalographically (27 letters)

The longest unhyphenated word in *Merriam-Webster's Collegiate Dictionary*, 10th ed.

antitransubstantiationalist (27 letters)

one who doubts that consecrated bread and wine actually change into the body and blood of Christ.

disproportionableness and **incomprehensibilities** (21 letters)

These are described by the *1992 Guinness Book of World Records* as the longest words in common usage.

Source: http://www.fun-with-words.com/word_longest.html

2

Computer Viruses Will Live Forever

In November 1988, I was sitting in Cornell's computer science labs working on a research project. Next to me, a grad student with bushy, brownish-red hair, wearing glasses, had his head down on the table, sleeping, I assumed. After about a half hour I peeked at his screen. "I miss you" was the only thing written in an open but otherwise blank e-mail.

A few days later, all the computers at Cornell went down. My mom, who was working at Siemens in New Jersey, called and told me all the computers at her place were down as well, and everyone was leaving work early. In fact, that day in November 1988, the first major Internet virus, dubbed the Internet Worm, brought down every computer connected to the Internet pretty much all over the world.

The next day, FBI agents were swarming the computer science department at Cornell. Turns out the student who had been sleeping at the computer next to me a week earlier, a guy named Robert Morris, had written the Internet Worm and unleashed it on the world, causing, as one headline suggested, $1 billion in lost productivity—

an amount I dispute, but given the extent to which the Internet has now taken over our lives, that figure would undoubtedly be much greater if a similar virus were unleashed today. Was it a malicious terrorist act, as some media suggested? It turns out it was simply a program gone awry, never intended to have the harmful effect that it did. And once the furor had died down, the papers went on to other, more important matters.

But this reminds me of the virus that tends to spread through the media every couple of weeks. This has been happening with stunning regularity since 1998 or so. It usually starts with some inane piece of economic data, such as the monthly jobs report. Perhaps, for instance, jobs (out of 100,000,000 jobs out there) were only up 98,000 last month (or any month) instead of the 115,000 that genius economists expected. The next thing you know, the markets are spiraling downward and pundits on TV and in the newspapers are whispering the R word. You know that word? The only thing worse are the D and S words (see end of this chapter). If there are two pieces of bad economic data, then those words inevitably start popping up. And then the virus starts: The markets in Shanghai go down because of R fears in the United States. And then everyone in the United States wakes up, sees Shanghai is down 10 percent, so Europe moves down 6 percent, U.S. futures are down 3 percent, and then Asia is down even more. It spreads like a contagion.

All of this ignores the fact that a month or two later, all the economic data is revised considerably. And instead of being up only 98,000 jobs, the number of new jobs is up 250,000. People laugh it off. "Oh, we were so silly that day two months earlier," but this virus repeats itself again and again. The only antidote to this sort of irrational behavior is to ask, Does it matter?

And to insulate your portfolio enough so that it doesn't.

Everyone assumes that the financial markets have to tank in a recession. But my feeling is, the stock market doesn't necessarily care if there's a recession. That's because of the following three things we know to be true:

- The Fed will start stimulating again in an actual recession, and rates will go down.
- Stocks get cheap, and many stocks trade below cash.
- Not every stock goes down in a recession.

To back this up, I took a look at all of the recessions since World War II.

First of all, I looked at yields on the ten-year note. Yields fell during ten of the eleven postwar recessions. The only time they didn't fall was the recession of November 1973 to March 1975, when the yield on the ten-year went from about 6.7 percent to 7.5 percent. So far, so good—I could use some lower yields.

By *yields*, I'm referring to the interest payment on the ten-year Treasury bills. The U.S. government uses Treasury bills when it borrows money. When people put their money in Treasury bills, they are lending the government money. Nothing is safer than that investment—we're all in a lot of trouble if the U.S. government defaults. When yields are very high (which tends to happen when there are inflation worries and the Federal Reserve raises rates), people are more inclined to put money in Treasury bills than in the stock market. Why take the risk on stocks when you can get a high interest payment on your Treasury bills? When rates are low, people are more inclined to put their money in assets that have a better return, like the stock market or real estate. Businesses are also more likely to borrow money and invest in growth because interest rates in general are low when T-bill rates are low. This spurs the economy and hence the stock market. This is why people usually like it when yields are low and why yields go down in a recession—to light a fire under the economy and pick things up again.

For the stock market, the data are a little more mixed. While we would expect recessions to be not great for stocks, they don't seem to be horrible either. Let's look at the last eleven recessions. The market has gone up during six of them (1945, 1953, 1960, 1980, 1981, and 1990) and down during five (1948, 1957, 1969, 1973, and 2001). On average, across all eleven, the market was dead flat.

Granted, eleven isn't a big number, and the volatility is quite large across the sample. The worst was a 22 percent drawdown during the 1973 recession, and the best was the 21 percent postwar bump during the 1945 recession.

Let's look instead at the initial story in this chapter—a real virus hitting the Internet. Even though it's twenty years later, the threat of another large-scale Internet virus, taking advantage of the hundreds of security loopholes that exist to this day on each of our personal computers, is still large enough that it's worthwhile to look at the public companies that stand to benefit from this threat.

CERT.org, part of the Software Engineering Institute at Carnegie Mellon University, catalogs the vulnerabilities introduced into commercial software that viruses and worms have been able to exploit each year. The number has gone from 3,784 in 2003 to 7,236 in 2007. This number is not going to go down, regardless of whether the United States or the world goes into a recession or depression. The success or failure of a company that protects against viruses is not going to depend on whether or not consumers can afford luxury Christmas gifts, but rather on companies' ability to identify the new viruses that are taking hold and develop software to counteract them. The way to find these companies is to keep track of which antivirus businesses are owned by the superinvestors, and which ones are consistently growing their cash stockpiles (so they can continue to do R & D) and book value per share.

For instance, Symantec (SYMC) is a good one to keep in mind. Symantec, like many good companies, was hit by a failed integration of an acquisition in 2005. The idea was right: Let's buy Veritas, a provider of storage software, because every corporation that needs to enhance their storage systems will also need to secure that stored data.

The integration, though, has gone slower than people thought it would, despite initial excitement about the idea, and the stock has flattened in the mid teens. However, what intrigues me is that it has faltered to the extent that high-quality value-oriented and activist hedge funds have been scooping up shares of the stock. The company, as of this writing, has a $15 billion market cap, almost $1 billion in net cash, and more than $1.5 billion in cash flows, giving it a multiple over cash flows of less than 10.

Thanks to the increasing need for protection against viruses, Symantec has been able to steadily grow sales, even in the middle of the great tech depression of 2000–02:

SYMANTEC SALES

Year Ending	Revenues (millions)
03/07	$5,199.37
03/06	$4,143.39
03/05	$2,582.85
03/04	$1,870.13
03/03	$1,406.95
03/02	$1,071.44
03/01	$853.55
03/00	$745.73
03/99	$592.63
03/98	$532.94

In addition, the list of investors who are buying up large numbers of shares of SYMC reads like a who's who of value investors. Carl Icahn lists the stock on his recent filings, as does deep-value investor Bruce Sherman of Private Capital. Extreme activist investor Bob Chapman of Chapman Capital has been accumulating it as well, although he hasn't actively called for change yet. This really is the forever play in the Internet virus space. Of course, anything can change by the time one reads this book. Chapman, for instance, might be long gone from the stock. But in general I like to pay attention to the moves of the successful hedge funds. Even if he's not in the stock at a later date, I can have confidence that his team has done its research on the company, the industry, and the true value of the stock. True, I don't have to believe everything he says, but it's a good starting point, particularly since we're identifying these stocks as being part of a larger demographic trend that will play out over the next fifty years.

Meanwhile, speaking of viruses, things did not end badly for our Internet Worm friend, Robert Morris. After dropping out of Cornell's grad school, doing his community service as sentenced by the judge, and staying out of trouble for a few years, he started Viaweb, a company that helped automate the process by which merchants could create online stores. He sold the company in 1998 to Yahoo! for $45 million, and it still exists to this day as Yahoo! Stores. He went on to obtain a PhD from Harvard, and he now has tenure at MIT. Not all terrible events have such a happy ending, but when the basic building blocks are there, good things can happen.

3

Inoculate Your Portfolio Against the Risk of Global Pandemic

I try to minimize doing things that can kill me. For instance, I don't skydive. Nor do I ski or play football while drunk. I won't even train to be a tightrope walker. I don't fly a plane because, for one thing, I don't even drive. So it's probably less safe for me to fly. In fact, I don't even like being a passenger on a plane if I can avoid it. People can get hurt doing things like that. It's not that I avoid taking all risks, it's just that I really like to live so my life is one thing I avoid risking.

Here's the problem, though: pandemics. Airborne illness. They're going to strike at some point, and they're a risk that there's really no way to protect against. I do try to wash my hands after riding a New York City subway, but that's a lot harder to do than, say, avoiding skydiving in the middle of the night. I was talking in early 2008 to the chief risk officer of a $5 billion fund of hedge funds. I was asking him if he was worried about subprime exposure, credit risk, and the like in the various hedge funds his fund was invested in. "Of course not," he said, "that was a risk we anticipated two years ago, and we stayed clear. You want to know what I spend every waking moment tracking now?"

"Of course," I said.

"Bird flu," he said. "Every day a pandemic doesn't happen increases the odds that the next day it will happen. And it will happen eventually."

So what happens in a global pandemic? Is there any way we can avoid it? The answer to the second question is maybe. At the very least, we can postpone it, which leads to some investment opportunities.

For the answer to the first question, we can look at the last major pandemic that swept the world. In the pandemic of Spanish flu of 1918, a variation on the influenza virus infected about one-fifth of the world's population. No big deal, right? It was only the flu. Isn't that just some coughing, a little fever, you sleep it off, and you're all better?

Not in this case: 50 million people died. If a pandemic like that hits again, it will be much worse, for a couple of reasons:

The rural-to-urban demographic trend is causing a larger number of more concentrated groups of people to be exposed to bacteria and infectious agents than ever before.

Extra-virulent strains of the flu are slowly evolving immunity to any type of treatment that can either prevent the disease or cure it once symptoms occur.

We've been lucky that the current flu is mostly innocuous. Up to 20 percent of the U.S. population contracts the flu every year. Even so, every year about forty thousand Americans die from it. Want to avoid the flu? Try to avoid being a child or older than sixty-five. Try to avoid prolonged stays in hospitals, where it's increasingly likely you'll be exposed to it. Don't smoke. Don't have kidney disease or any chronic illness. Try to avoid aspirin. Don't get pregnant. Of course, even without any of these factors, you still might get the flu. I just recovered from it and I'm none of the above.

With a disease like chicken pox, after you've contracted it, it's unlikely you'll ever get it again, because your body develops antibodies that protect you against it in the future. So how is it possible to suffer from the flu every year? Well, you actually don't get the same flu every year. The flu is like the Borg on *Star Trek*. It assimilates us. It evolves and changes itself to overcome the immunities we build each year. Most of the time these changes in the flu virus (specifically, in the proteins that make up the surface of the virus) are minor modifications and don't drastically affect the consequences of being infected. But a significant change could, and will eventually, occur. From the World Health Organization Web site:

> When a major change in either one or both of their surface proteins occurs spontaneously, no one will have partial or full immunity against infection because it is a completely new virus. If this new virus also has the capacity to spread from person-to-person, then a pandemic will occur.
>
> Outbreaks of influenza in animals, especially when happening simultaneously with annual outbreaks in humans, increase the chances of a pandemic, through the merging of animal and human influenza viruses. During the last few years, the world has faced several threats with pandemic potential, making the occurrence of the next pandemic just a matter of time.
>
> If an influenza pandemic appears, we could expect the following:
> - Given the high level of global traffic, the pandemic virus may spread rapidly, leaving little or no time to prepare.
> - Vaccines, antiviral agents and antibiotics to treat secondary infections will be in short supply and will be unequally distributed. It will take several months before any vaccine becomes available.
> - Medical facilities will be overwhelmed.

- Widespread illness may result in sudden and potentially significant shortages of personnel to provide essential community services.
- The effect of influenza on individual communities will be relatively prolonged when compared to other natural disasters, as it is expected that outbreaks will reoccur.

One way to prepare against a pandemic is to not only monitor, and quarantine when potential outbreaks appear, but also develop the appropriate vaccines to deal with variations of all the diseases that could reach pandemic status.

Do vaccines work? Yes, they likely save millions of lives, although evaluating them can be complicated. For example, you must look carefully at conditions before and after widespread use of the vaccine. Even if there's a huge reduction in occurrences of the disease, you also have to see if there were other changes in the affected area's infrastructure (for instance, the development of clean-water systems) that could have also reduced occurrence of a disease. There's also the question of what happens if a disease is completely eradicated but a country continues to vaccinate all its children. In this case, it's possible that new occurrences of the disease could be directly related to use of the vaccine, which is a modified, ineffective version of the pathogen that's injected in order to promote antibody development. In general, it's clear that vaccines work, but there are other issues involved that are open to debate and possible future investments.

The United States has been very fortunate. It's been able to inoculate most of its population against all vaccine-preventable diseases, from tuberculosis to polio and now even the basic flu. Given the success we've had, many developing countries are now adopting similar guidelines: that every child in grades K–12 should be inoculated against as many diseases as there are vaccines for. This mandate is still spreading throughout the world and is increasing demand for the vaccines developed by the companies mentioned below.

However, many third-world countries haven't been as lucky as we. There is an economic disincentive for companies to develop vaccines for these countries—they're poorer, so they spend less. It's estimated that more than 2 million children die every year from diseases that could have been prevented by currently available vaccines. The Bill & Melinda Gates Foundation has devoted hundreds of millions of dollars to bringing that number down. This money is going toward developing new vaccines for widespread diseases like malaria, AIDS, diabetes, and others, as well as toward improving distribution of existing vaccines.

In addition, recent innovations have allowed companies to develop potential vaccines for cancer. These vaccines don't work in the same way as others. Without getting too technical, a cancer vaccine usually would be administered *after* someone is diagnosed. A sample of the tumor is used to develop cells that will fight the growth of that particular malignancy in that individual's body.

Vaccines, then, have a fourfold investment potential:

Fast-food chains tend to go national after focusing on a specific region. Starbucks (SBUX) is a perfect example of this regional-to-national growth, having spread throughout the country after it first came public, beginning in the Northwest. Similarly, vaccines are spreading from the United States to the rest of the world.

The fear of a pandemic is increasing the amount of research money devoted to vaccines, as well as the government-sponsored stockpiles that are created when any new vaccine comes to market.

Money is being poured into the "forgotten diseases" in countries ignored until now that couldn't afford to do medical research or to provide the economic incentive to companies that could do the research.

Novel technologies for potential cancer vaccines could end up developing a new trillion-dollar industry.

Let's look at a variety of companies that deal in these various investment scenarios. Since our goal is to sleep soundly at night, we'll be sure to check the first box: We'll bet on a demographic trend that is not going away and will inevitably increase over the next fifty years. We need to find companies that have demonstrated consistent growth, have a good investor base (it's always nice if Warren Buffett is on our side), and have a good balance sheet (lots of cash is a good thing). For the smaller, more speculative research companies, we also need to make sure they are diversified.

One of my favorite companies in the vaccine sector is Invitrogen (IVGN).

INVITROGEN CORP.

as of Apr. 23, 2008

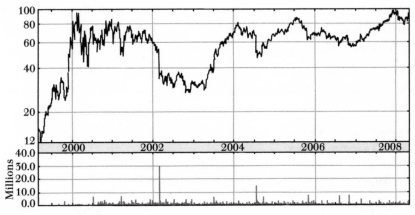

This company has the essential building blocks that pharmaceutical companies and research institutions need in order to research new vaccines. It does drug discovery, genomics, gene analysis, and diagnostics. It's not worth doing an analysis of its P/E ratios, because this is intended to be a forever portfolio, but at the time of this writing, Invitrogen has become extremely cheap, with a forward P/E of just 12, while at the same time improving margins, cash flows, and revenues. The expertise this company provides will always be needed by the entire industry to develop new vaccines.

Additionally, I like the fact that the value fund Perry Capital is a long-term shareholder of the company, as is Blue Harbour Capital, a hedge fund run by an ex-KKR executive, KKR being the premier private-equity buyout fund ever.

Next, it's worth looking at the biotech company Genzyme (GENZ), which makes treatments for rare genetic disorders and products for organ transplants. What's good for the purposes of this chapter is that it is also developing cancer vaccines.

Many of the companies developing such vaccines (such as Dendreon and Genitope) are very speculative and thus too risky to recommend for a long-term portfolio. Those speculative companies have nothing else going on other than their FDA trials, which may or may not succeed. GENZ, though, offers many products that have already been in the marketplace, are generating hundreds of millions in cash flows, and provide the balance sheet and stability needed as a foundation for finding the next trillion-dollar industry. GENZ is the bet that these cancer vaccines will eventually take off.

GENZYME CORP.

as of Apr. 23, 2008

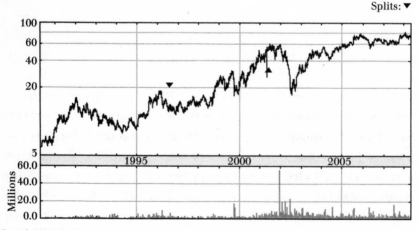

Still, with all of these stocks, it's worth noting that there's volatility. For instance, in 2002, GENZ dipped along with the rest of the market before nicely recovering. But in 2000–01, when there was a horrible bear market and recession, not to mention the terrorist attacks, GENZ was at all-time highs, a situation it similarly finds itself in at the time of this writing, despite fears of a global financial credit crisis.

BAXTER INTERNATIONAL, INC.
as of Apr. 23, 2008

Splits: ▼

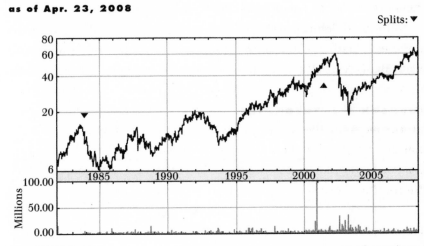

Copyright 2008 Yahoo! Inc.   http://finance.yahoo.com

Baxter International (BAX) is another way you can access a solid cash flow–generating company that provides a wide variety of products and services in the biotech and health-care sectors, but at the same time get a backdoor into a potentially enormous vaccine market. The list of diseases that Baxter provides treatments and services for includes hemophilia, immune disorders, cancer, infectious diseases, and renal disease. However, our backdoor interest here is that it is developing a SARS vaccine. SARS and related flus are eventually going to hit with a vengeance. BAX has the balance sheet, the solid investor base, and the enormous cash flows generated by its other product lines to spend the resources developing the new industry that SARS will create. Let's not forget that a flu pandemic, in addition to potentially causing up to 10 million deaths or more worldwide, will also cause up to 150 million hospital visits. Though this would be a horrible event, an investment like BAX will allow me to sleep easier, particularly if I'm sick with bird flu.

It's also comforting to know that Relational Investors, run by Ralph Whitworth (at the time of this writing, Whitworth just became an activist investor in Sprint-Nextel), is one of the largest shareholders of BAX. If he's comfortable owning almost $2 billion worth of the stock (as of early 2008), then I am also.

Johnson & Johnson (JNJ) is one of the largest health-care firms out there, with $61 billion in revenues. It's a maker of everything from Band-Aids to Tylenol to medicines for countless other illnesses.

JOHNSON & JOHNSON, INC.
as of Apr. 23, 2008

Splits: ▼

Copyright 2008 Yahoo! Inc.   http://finance.yahoo.com

Why do I like it? The company is making a vaccine for hepatitis B. Oh, and Warren Buffett keeps increasing his holdings in the company and owns more than $4 billion worth of the stock. I don't like taking risks, but at least I know he's taking a bigger risk than I am.

BARR PHARMACEUTICALS, INC.

as of Apr. 23, 2008

Splits: ▼

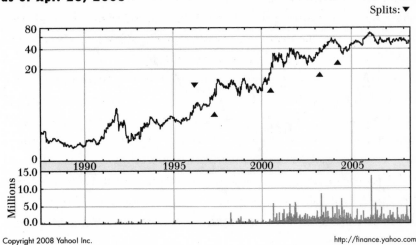

Copyright 2008 Yahoo! Inc.   http://finance.yahoo.com

Barr Pharmaceuticals (BRL) is another general pharmaceutical company of the JNJ variety, but on a smaller scale, with $2.6 billion in revenues. In addition to drugs to treat a hundred illnesses, the company is also developing, for the U.S. government, a vaccine to treat adenovirus, a particular type of flu that tends to affect up to 30 percent of military personnel a year and rapidly spreads through confined spaces like military barracks.

Netherlands-based company Crucell (CRXL) makes liquid vaccines for a variety of childhood diseases, as well as vaccines for typhoid, cholera, hepatitis A and B, and others. In addition, it licenses its technology to other research companies that are developing vaccines. I also like the fact that a variety of superinvestors own the stock: Renaissance Technologies, Moore Capital, DE Shaw, and Citadel. You can't find a better lineup. This investor base can change at any given moment, but these guys own big stakes, and they are certainly making a bet on the potential of the vaccines that Crucell is developing.

CRUCELL N.V. ADS
as of Apr. 23, 2008

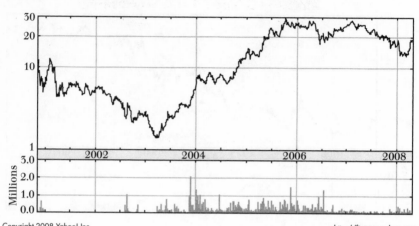

I like the companies mentioned above for creating a forever portfolio, but it's also worth mentioning a very creative exchange-traded fund (ETF) set up by the specialists at Claymore, an ETF provider, and at Clear Asset Management, a maker of specialty indices. The fund is called the Global Vaccine ETF (JNR). It invests across the spectrum of the ETF industry. See page 35 for its top holdings as of April 23, 2008:

TOP FUND HOLDINGS AS OF FEBRUARY 14, 2008

Name	Weighting
CSI Ltd.	6.50 %
Invitrogen Corp.	6.15 %
Genzyme Corp.	5.83 %
Baxter International, Inc.	5.38 %
Johnson & Johnson, Inc.	5.24 %
Barr Pharmaceuticals, Inc.	4.97 %
Merck & Co., Inc.	4.93 %
Sanofi-Aventis	4.88 %
Novartis AG ADR	4.78 %
Takeda Chemical Industries	4.68 %
Dow Chemical Co.	4.47 %
Pfizer Inc.	4.38 %
Solvay SA	4.31 %
GlaxoSmithKline Plc-ADR	4.21 %
Bristol-Myers Squibb Co.	4.03 %
Wyeth	3.63 %
Medarex, Inc.	3.34 %
Crucell N.V. ADS	3.24 %
Dendreon Corp.	2.61 %
Progenics Pharmaceuticals, Inc.	2.11 %
Geron Corp.	1.92 %
Cytos Biotechnology AG	1.23 %
Novavax, Inc.	0.83 %
Cell Genesys, Inc.	0.77 %
Transgene SA	0.73 %

The great thing about investing in the vaccine space, particularly with the companies described above, is that it allows you to take advantage of several overlapping trends:

- **Baby Boomers retiring.** Several of the companies mentioned, particularly JNJ, BAX, and GENZ, deal with many of the illnesses and treatments that will be required for the retiring Baby Boomer demographic as they age.
- **The clean-water/global-warming trend.** This is also related to the trend of rural-to-urban that is happening throughout the developing third world. As people are in increasingly close quarters, with potentially filthier conditions and less access to clean running water, disease will spread.
- **The vaccine trend with the premises mentioned above,** particularly with countries pledging more money to vaccine research.

To invest in these trends, with the comfort of knowing you are in solid companies with great investors at your side, allows you to escape the fear that any marked episodes of market volatility, recession, or inflation will cause you undue anxiety. As we all know, stress can wreak havoc on your immune system.

4

Diamonds, Clothes, Chocolate

LIVE THE GOOD LIFE

I've never before written about what I'm going to tell you, and there are a few reasons why:

- It might appear like bragging, in a perverse sort of way;
- There's a shame factor, for various reasons;
- And it perhaps will destroy my credibility with some of my readers.

But in the summer of 2000, during the worst part of the dot-com bust, I lost about a million dollars a week for the entire summer. And no, it wasn't some investors' money. It was my own. Well, so what? Everyone lost a lot of money then. I had sold my first company for stock in another company that eventually went bankrupt. That company was Xceed, Inc. Some of my losses were due to that ill-fated decision to trade my company in for what would become a worthless corporation. But also part of it was simply due to the fact that I had never experienced a bear market—or anything but a strong positive arc over my entire career.

When you constantly succeed in life, it's hard to recognize adversity even when it hits you right in the face. Eventually, I lost an enormous amount of money. I also ended up losing my apartment in TriBeCa—4,500 square feet on the top floor. The elevator opened directly into the living room, where the first thing one saw upon entering the apartment was an antique pool table (I lost that, too) and several thousand books lining bookshelves that went from the floor to the twenty-foot-high ceilings (most of those books are still in storage or have been given away).

When the apartment was put up for sale, Christy Turlington, the model best known for representing Calvin Klein, was one of the first to look at it. After that, I garnered a reputation among high-end real-estate agents for sticking too close to potential buyers, and as a result, I was asked to vacate the premises anytime a buyer was coming over. So I missed out on meeting Julianne Moore, Harvey Keitel, and one guy who never gave his name and was arrested by the FBI the second he left my apartment building.

How did I lose all that money? Did I spend it? Of course not. It's hard to spend a million dollars a week, although I did try and I'm assuming there are people out there who successfully do it. I will admit this now: I had no clue whatsoever about investing and how to manage risk. I did not construct a forever portfolio for myself. Instead, I only made a "today portfolio" each day. I would load up on any stock I thought was going to go up that day, 1999 style, and hope for the best. Even thinking about it now, I feel sick to my stomach. After my investments disappeared, my family wanted me to sue my stockbroker. But he was a good guy and certainly did not need to take responsibility for decisions that were completely my own.

For years I lamented losing that money. After selling my place in Manhattan, I basically sentenced myself to exile, moved upstate, and only bit by bit came out of my shell and built my finances—and myself—back up. I swore to myself I would not allow this to ever happen to me again. So I studied the investment business like there was no tomorrow, to make sure I would never make the same mistakes. I successfully traded for several hedge funds. Then I started a fund of hedge funds, and finally founded the social networking site for investing, Stockpickr.com. Along the way, I did various M & A deals as well as private equity investments that turned out well.

All of this is a roundabout way of saying that in 1999 I should've stopped trading and bought myself and my family things that could have made our lives better—perhaps more paintings, an incredible wine collection, or a nice car. No matter how much I spent on luxury goods, I never would have spent as much money as I ended up losing. And, look, losing money is not the worst thing that can happen to someone. It forced me to learn the investment business. It allowed me to gain perspective on life in ways that I would not have otherwise. Now that I am in a brand-new chapter of my life, I can write this book with the hope that readers will gain the valuable insights that I lacked back in 1999, and avoid making the mistakes that cost me many millions of dollars.

In hindsight, I should have spent like a drunken sailor. I should have indulged myself and bought anything I wanted. However, there is an upside. Not only do I have the opportunity again, but so will many of the readers of this book. The worldwide luxury industry is booming. And it doesn't matter if there's a subprime credit crisis in the United States, a recession, or even a depression. Every year there are more millionaires across the globe than the year before. The number of households with cash assets of more than $1 million (that excludes real estate) has doubled from 4.5 million in 1996 to 10 million in 2007. The global net worth of these millionaires is expected to increase from $37 trillion in 2008 to $52 trillion in 2011, according to an analysis by the consulting firm Capgemini.

As the net worth of these individuals continues to grow, the consumption of luxury goods will also grow. According to the Telsey

Advisory Group, the size of the global luxury-goods industry is $150 billion. This number is only going to increase over the next fifty years for several reasons:

- **Global net worth is increasing.**
- **It's another aftereffect of the rural-to-urban trend discussed throughout this book.** As third-world cities become centers of commerce, this introduces new markets for luxury goods, as well as home bases for newly minted millionaires.
- **The luxury companies have continuously become more sophisticated in using the high-end powers of their branding** to sell products to middle-income customers. Dana Thomas's book *Deluxe: How the Luxury Industry Lost Its Luster* describes the origins of this trend in detail, but a great example is how superfashion brand Christian Dior eventually got into the T-shirt business (with J'adore Dior printed on the shirts) to market its brand to everyone.

This is an industry that's surprisingly recession independent. High-net-worth families are less sticker-sensitive, so luxury-goods companies have more pricing power. And unlike lower-income spenders, high-net-worth spending does not fluctuate with the unemployment rate.

In other words, the fastest growth in the demographic we are looking at (high-net-worth consumers who buy luxury items) is not happening in the United States, but in South Korea, India, Russia, and other Asian and Middle Eastern countries. A recession in the United States, while not pleasant for anyone, will not affect the luxury industry as much as one would think.

There are several ways to play the rise in the global wealth industry. For one thing, as the number of families worth $1 million increases, the need for advisers increases. Wealthy families need assistance with everything from taxes to estate planning to investing—even art collecting. High-end banks like Goldman Sachs (GS) and Credit

Suisse First Boston (CS) are the top two for dealing with this blossoming trend.

GOLDMAN SACHS GROUP, INC.
as of Apr. 23, 2008

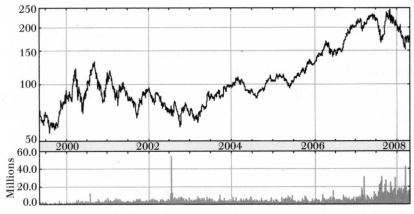

Copyright 2008 Yahoo! Inc. http://finance.yahoo.com

Goldman Sachs is sometimes called a glorified hedge fund because so much of its profit comes from its trading business. Goldman has avoided any lines of business that tend to be most affected by global downturns. It isn't a retail stockbroker, it doesn't do credit cards, and it's not big in the mutual-fund business. And, I can tell you from my own experience, you need a very large number to be welcomed with open arms by Goldman's wealth-management division (note: I'm not a Goldman customer).

Let's not forget the conspiracy theories on Goldman Sachs. Because of Goldman's emphasis on its employees engaging in some form of public service, the Goldman management team, for better or worse, has taken this to an extreme. Here are some former Goldman execs who have ended up more or less ruling the world:

Robert Rubin, former secretary of the Treasury
Hank Paulson, current secretary of the Treasury
Robert Zoellick, president of the World Bank

Jon Corzine, governor of New Jersey

Joshua Bolten, White House chief of staff

Kenneth Brody, former president of the Export-Import Bank of
the United States

Steven Friedman, former director of the National Economic
Council

And the list goes on. I don't want to get into conspiracy theories here, but if you're a very affluent individual looking for a place to put your money, this is a good bet. I don't believe it's possible to find a safer stock for the next fifty years than GS.

A MILLION-DOLLAR BONUS

So it was a big day for my friend Mike. He had just gotten his bonus and the total was all in for 2007. He had made $1 million. We met for lunch. "Congratulations," I told him, "you're a millionaire now."

"I know," he said, "it's my first million. I hope I make more, though, next year, because this is ridiculous."

"What do you mean? It's a million dollars. Doesn't that put you in the top 0.001 percent of the entire human race in terms of salary?"

"Ugh. Whatever. I'll be lucky if I'm not broke by this time next year."

"C'mon, you never made money like this before. Now you just made a million dollars. How can you spend it that quickly?"

"Well, first off," he explained, "half of that million is in deferred stock compensation. So I vest into it over the next five years if I stay at the bank." (Mike is a VP at a top-tier bank.) "So I sort of have that money but I can't spend it, and who the hell stays at a job for five years? I'm going to have to figure out how to get someone to pay me a signing bonus eventually that matches what I'm giving up. And if the economy goes south, what guarantees do I have?

"Second, out of the half a million that's left, count off half to the IRS. That's

$250K left. My wife wants to upgrade our Hamptons rental. Throw out another $50K for next summer. I have one kid in kindergarten and another in second grade. When you count private school tuition, ballet, and fencing lessons—that's at least another $60K out the window. So now I have $140K."

Mike, and I'm not exaggerating, loosened his tie. He was having trouble breathing.

"OK, so now I have about $12K a month left here. Well, my mortgage is five thousand dollars a month, and don't think I can sell my twelve-hundred-square-foot apartment that I bought for $1.4 million two years ago, because where am I going to move? Brooklyn? Believe me, the prices don't get any better there, and all the partners live in Manhattan. No Manhattan, no partnership. So now I have $7K a month left. And I don't mean to sound like a snob or anything, but I do have a housekeeper, babysitters, gym memberships, therapists for me and my wife, plus our couples therapist. I don't know where it goes every month, but I know my credit card is being used to pay for it. James, I don't know how to do it.

"Meanwhile, the job is crazy right now. We're pitching every deal out there, and every private equity firm is right in there competing with us. We're all using the same playbooks, and the deals keep getting ratcheted up, but now nobody can get any loans to close a deal. Who knows what bonuses will be next year. It's a nightmare out there."

We then sat there for a few minutes without saying a word. I had known Mike for fifteen years. Every Monday night back in the midnineties, we used to go to comedy night at the Luna Lounge on Ludlow Street on the Lower East Side. Up-and-coming comedians would perform, and every now and then some of those comedians would eventually break out with their own show on Comedy Central or a standup show on HBO. It was exciting to see, and after the shows we'd always go to El Hat to eat Mexican food. When Mike got married, he wanted to pay for the wedding himself, which meant he could invite only his parents, his bride's parents, and a few friends, including me (although I was out of town that weekend and had to pass).

A few years later, when he was an associate at the first bank he was working at, he celebrated for a week when he got his first $50,000 cash bonus. It was during dot-com days and everything was heady. He put it into a wireless highflier and watched it double, which allowed him to buy his first apartment. Life was good, and it seemed then as though it would last forever.

"I just have to work harder this year," he suddenly said. "I've gotta really break out of the grind somehow, or else the pressure is going to break my back, you know what I mean?"

"Well, listen. I wish you were happier with this. Can you quit the rat race somehow? It sounds like it's stressing you out."

"Are you kidding? And do what? Make a measly $250K at some chop-shop? Sell toothpaste for Procter & Gamble? I work seventy hours a week, man. I deserve every penny of what I've got."

Not every luxury company is about diamonds or managing money. People value their eyesight, the ability to see is good, but looking good while you see is just as important.

LUXOTTICA GROUP SPA
as of Apr. 23, 2008

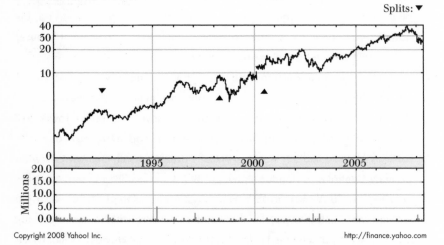

Splits: ▼

It's hard to find a long-term chart less volatile than Luxottica Group (LUX), and for good reason. This company makes basically every luxury brand of eyeglasses and sunglasses, including Ray-Ban,

Rēvo, Arnette, Killer Loop, Persol, Vogue, Luxottica, and Sferoflex; as well as designer lines such as Prada, Chanel, Miu Miu, Dolce & Gabbana, Versace, Versus, Bulgari, Salvatore Ferragamo, Donna Karan, DKNY, Brooks Brothers, Anne Klein, Burberry, Polo, Ralph Lauren, and Puma. And its wholesale line is mostly recession independent—you need to see clearly, even when the market's heading down.

TIFFANY & CO.
as of Apr. 23, 2008

Copyright 2008 Yahoo! Inc.   http://finance.yahoo.com

The high-end jewelry business is booming along with the growth of developing Asia. In the 2007 holiday season, Tiffany (TIF) experienced 29 percent growth in this region versus a 2 percent decline in the United States. In fact, 50 percent of TIF's revenues come from overseas, and that percentage will continue to increase. In addition, 25 percent of its revenues come from the engagement and wedding business. As long as people continue to get married, this business, backed by the Tiffany's brand and its instantly recognizable blue box, will continue to do well.

Activist investor and former corporate raider Nelson Peltz is one of the largest shareholders of Tiffany at the time of this writing. So far he hasn't stated his activist intentions, but Peltz has done an excellent job of spotting undervalued opportunities and riding them to their fullest. He has previously been a large shareholder in both Wendy's and H. J. Heinz. And while diamonds aren't exactly ketchup, Peltz has an excellent eye for detecting areas of a company that management could improve in order to bring up shareholder value. Peltz tends to also be a very focused, long-term investor. Currently, he owns Heinz, Wendy's, Tiffany, and Chemtura (CEM).

Chemtura, incidentally, is an interesting company to look at for a forever portfolio. It manufactures specialty chemicals for a wide variety of industries. Among other things, its products are used in water-purification processes, and thus are related to the themes on clean water mentioned in chapter 10.

COACH, INC.
as of Apr. 23, 2008

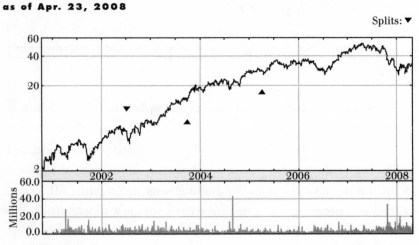

Splits: ▼

Copyright 2008 Yahoo! Inc.   http://finance.yahoo.com

Coach, Inc. (COH) is another popular luxe brand that deserves consideration. It is a maker of men's and women's accessories, including handbags, scarves, jackets, sweaters, gloves, and jewelry.

CHOCOLATE VERSUS VANILLA

A chapter on affluent spending can't just rest with clothes, cars, and banking; the very important topic of high-end candy must be included. If we're talking trends, then the trend of ever-increasing chocolate consumption (see also chapter 8 on obesity) cannot be ignored. The average American eats ten pounds of chocolate a year. This number is expected to rise to thirteen pounds a year by 2012. The average Swiss person consumes more than double that—twenty-one pounds of chocolate a year. Why do the Swiss eat so much more than Americans? Well, the chocolate is better there, and people have easy access to high-quality brands. Almost every human likes chocolate, and if you have good chocolate around, you're going to eat it. For our forever portfolio, however, let's look at who doesn't have easy access to chocolate but soon will: the Chinese. The average Chinese citizen eats less than one-half pound of chocolate a year. As the rural-to-urban trend increases in China and as the middle class continues to grow, demand for chocolate should skyrocket even faster than the demand for commodities with industrial uses, like oil.

Ten Facts About Chocolate

1. The earliest documented use of chocolate was approximately 1100 B.C.
2. The Mayans and Aztecs made chocolate beverages.
3. It is associated with the Mayan god and Aztec goddess of fertility.
4. It can affect serotonin levels in the brain.
5. It can lower blood pressure.
6. It has a substantial amount of antioxidants that reduce the formation of free radicals.
7. In ancient times, cacao beans were used as currency.
8. Two-thirds of the world's cocoa is produced in western Africa.

9. The Ivory Coast produces 43 percent of all the cocoa.
10. Worldwide, 50 million people depend on cocoa as a source of livelihood, according to the World Cocoa Foundation.

Considering these kinds of statistics, it's only natural to include an assortment of chocolate in a forever portfolio. Hershey Foods (HSY) is a large chocolate and confectionery company—one of the biggest in the world—made famous by its ubiquitous Hershey bars. Because the demand for chocolate is almost as consistent as that for electricity, chocolate companies always pay a high yield. HSY currently yields 3.3 percent, and it has never cut that dividend.

THE HERSHEY COMPANY
as of Apr. 23, 2008

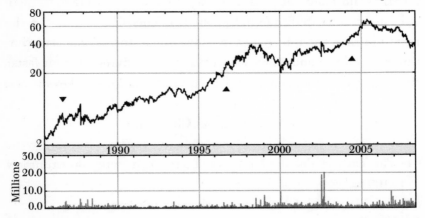

Splits: ▼

Copyright 2008 Yahoo! Inc.   http://finance.yahoo.com

Cadbury Schweppes plc (CSG) is a London-based confectionery and beverage company that was founded in 1783. Some of their products include cocoa powder and milk chocolate bars. The stock has a yield of 2.5 percent.

CADBURY SCHWEPPES PLC ADRS
as of Apr. 23, 2008

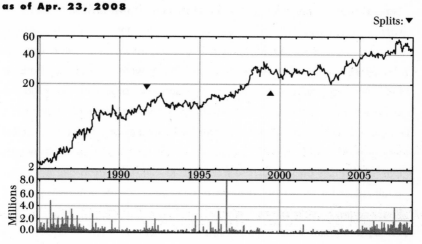

Splits: ▼

Copyright 2008 Yahoo! Inc.   http://finance.yahoo.com

There are several other, lesser-known plays worth consider-ing. Rocky Mountain Chocolate Factory (RMCF) is a very low-cap Colorado-based company that makes and markets chocolate and candy, including caramels, creams, mints, and truffles. The stock has a yield of 3.5 percent.

Tootsie Roll Industries (TR) makes all kinds of candy, including Tootsie Rolls, Tootsie Roll Pops, Caramel Apple Pops, Charms, Blow Pops, Blue Razz, Zip-a-Dee Pops, Cella's Chocolate-Covered Cher-ries, Mason Dots, Crows (formerly Mason Black Crows), Junior Mints, Charleston Chew, Sugar Daddy, and Sugar Babies. The stock has a yield of 1.3 percent.

The J. M. Smucker Co. (SJM), in addition to making Smucker's preserves, also distributes dessert and ice cream toppings, such as its Chocolate-Mocha Spoonable Ice Cream Topping and Chocolate Sun-dae Syrup. The stock has a yield of 2.5 percent.

THE COST OF VANILLA

No discussion of chocolate would be complete without mention of the great vanilla wars, particularly in light of the ultrainflation that's hit the price of oil. This is an important topic for me (I'll always choose a vanilla milkshake over chocolate) and for a forever portfolio. As people watch asset prices explode for different commodities, it's important to see how, over time, the world adjusts and prices react accordingly. The price of vanilla is a great example.

From 2000, when Cyclone Hudah hit Madagascar (the world's largest producer of vanilla), to 2002, when the island nation was engulfed by civil war, spot prices on vanilla rose from $25 to $400 per kilogram. It was no small matter for food manufacturers dependent on the world's most popular flavoring (most chocolate contains vanilla).

What happens when a supply shock like this occurs? The world economy steps in and develops solutions:

- Other countries where it was previously cost-prohibitive to commercially cultivate vanilla began producing it: Uganda, Papua New Guinea, India, and Indonesia.
- New technology developed that made synthetic vanillin (produced, incidentally, as a by-product of petroleum production) tastier. The use of synthetic vanillin went from 90 percent of the vanilla market to 97 percent of the market.
- New techniques are being developed using hydroponics that would allow vanilla (one of the most difficult crops to cultivate) to be grown in the United States and Europe.

All of this drove the price of vanilla down to where it is in 2008—about $125 per kilogram. The same phenomenon will occur, on a global scale, in oil.

Alternatives in technology to improve the drilling and refining process, a large number of small-caps and micro-caps getting funding to drill where it was previously too expensive, as well as increased spending on alternative fuels are going to rapidly increase supply and lower demand for crude over the next ten years. The same arc that occurred in vanilla—and has occurred in every commodity since time began—is going to occur with oil.

5

Common Sense Always Works

S ome years back, I was breakfasting at the Four Seasons with people representing a family that had built their fortune sometime between the fifteenth and seventeenth centuries and had managed to let it accumulate into tens of billions of dollars in Swiss banks. They were evaluating the latest wave of emerging hedge funds.

"We just saw an amazing hedge fund," one gentleman said to me. "The guys worked on the space shuttle and spent $2 million taking their stochastic vibration analysis techniques and using them to dominate the markets. They have over fifty computers running algorithms."

"Stop," I said. "Have you read the papers lately about the space shuttle?" referring to Lisa Nowak, the notorious NASA "diaper woman."

Everyone laughed.

"Seriously, whatever they are telling you about vibration analysis is a sham. Maybe they are legit, I have no idea. But nobody needs to spend $2 million developing space shuttle vibration techniques to beat the markets. That's just marketing. That's their pitch to get people suckered into giving them their money. It's like when academics in the late eighties built 'neural networks' to detect space missiles so that they could get funding for Star Wars research from the Defense Department. There's no such thing as a neural network. It's basic statistics with a fancy name on it. It was all just marketing."

By way of contrast, here's an example of a simple system that historically has done well in both bull and bear markets and does not apply any quantum mechanics or chaos theory. It takes advantage of the fact that the so-called dumb money tends to pile into (or pull out of) a stock when a trend has played out.

About five years ago, a specialist on the New York Stock Exchange taught me this trick. He said that if a company has bad news, wait three days, then buy. I tested the system on all the Nasdaq 100 stocks over the past ten years. In order to avoid suvivorship bias, I included stocks that had been deleted, and I took commissions into account.

While this book is about constructing a forever portfolio that allows you to never worry about your stock choices again, it's worth mentioning that there are some simple, common-sense systems that consistently work, year in and year out, for more active trading in both types of markets. If day trading strikes your fancy, consider a variation on a system like this: If a stock is down three straight days, buy the next morning at the open. If you own a stock and it's up two days in a row, sell it the next day at the open.

The idea behind this is that trends run out fast. After two consecutive days up, it is reasonable to expect a stock to slow down. After three down days in a row, all of the sellers are done. This is not always true. Often a stock goes down many more days than three. When it does, in this system, you buy more. But if it goes up two days in a row, you sell.

Furthermore, if you want to do risk management, do not use a stop-loss. An investor using a stop-loss takes a stock position and says,

"If I lose 10 percent, then I'm going to sell this position and stop my losses." Instead, it's better to keep position sizes small enough so that you never have to worry while you sleep at night about any one position. Stop-losses will almost always degrade the results of any system. You have to give it a chance to play out. If you're nervous about a stock going down 50 percent, keep position sizes small and make as many trades as possible.

I simulation-tested this system from 1997 to 2007, using only 2 percent of equity per trade. In the ten-year period, there were 16,777 instances when this method triggered a trade; of these, 10,706, or 64 percent, resulted in profitable trades. The average return per trade, counting winners and losers, was +1.93 percent, and the average holding period was six days. There were no down years. Bull-market years performed better, with a 200 percent result for 1999 in the simulation, but the bear market years 2000 and 2001 returned 40 percent and 80 percent, respectively, and even 2002 returned 3 percent. Long-only, mean-reversion systems love volatility, and these bear markets had a lot of volatility.

Should you play this system? I don't know. It's at least worth studying, especially before anyone sells you on a $2 million system. It seems as good as anything else.

Should you sell short using this system? A *short* is the opposite of buying. When you short a stock at $20, and it goes down to $15, then you made $5 while all the people who own the stock lost $5. It's a good way to go if you want to bet against the market. If a stock goes up two days in a row, why just sell? Why not short?

I tested a variation on this. Let's say the QQQQ (the ETF representing the Nasdaq 100) goes up two straight days, and the next morning it gaps up (the stock opens higher than the prior day's close) in what I call the sweet spot—between 0.3 and 0.6 percent. To short this sweet spot, either hold until the close or (not to be greedy) take profits if the QQQQ goes down 0.5 percent. Simple—no chaos theory necessary.

There have been seventy-one occurrences within this sweet-spot range since the QQQQ opened for trading in April 1999. Of these, sixty-five (92 percent) were successful, for an average gain of 0.36 percent. Bull or bear market, this approach has generated positive returns every year.

Note that these are short-term trading techniques as opposed to being components of a forever portfolio. However, one aspect of a forever portfolio is having a miniportfolio of shorter-term techniques that can be used when the markets are particularly volatile.

Common sense also suggests buying companies that are buying back their shares.

One of the wisest sayings I've heard is that when someone gives you an excuse for not doing something, "there's always a good reason, and then there's the real reason."

If, for example, someone does not want to shovel snow on the sidewalk, he may say, "Let's wait for the sun to come out and have the snow melt a little. Besides, it might snow again, so I should wait." Those are both sound reasons for not shoveling. But the real reason is he's too tired and would rather be inside watching TV.

The same thing happens with permabear pundits. For instance, there has been debate lately about whether or not the increase in share buybacks is good for corporate America. A share buyback occurs when a company decides its stock price is below what it should be and buys back its own stock on the open market. In the ideal scenario, shares outstanding go down and the shareholders benefit when earnings per share (and potential dividends per share) go up.

The permabear criticism of this is: Companies don't know what to do with their money because there are no longer good uses for it out there. The real reason they say this is: I'm a permabear and I need to find some weird way of saying that something that is enormously good for shareholders is bad.

Jim Cramer, in his book *Mad Money*, mentions a metric other than share buybacks that is useful for determining whether a stock is a buy: Look at companies that not only are buying back shares now but have also bought back significant amounts of stock in the past.

The first company worth looking at is IBM (IBM). A big criticism of share buybacks is that they are just used to counterbalance the increase in shares that results from giving employees stock options. However, IBM significantly decreased shares last year because of its buyback. Shares outstanding at the end of 2006 were 1.6 billion, down 4.6 percent from the year before. IBM bought back 97 million shares during the year and plans to continue buying back more, which it has been doing since 1995, to add to the 1.2 billion shares bought back since then. And the company has made an average of 50 percent on every purchase, since the average price is $62. In other words, IBM seems to be a good investor to piggyback.

What I find intriguing is that among IBM's large shareholders is Intel Capital, which invests Intel's money. Certainly Intel has insight into who is buying what in technology. IBM trades at only 13 times 2007 expected earnings. It's buying back its own company hand over fist, and has a 30 percent return on equity—meaning that every additional dollar it puts to work generates 30¢ in earnings, so it's a smart allocator of capital.

MORE REASONS IBM IS SUITABLE
FOR THE FOREVER PORTFOLIO

In 1991, I blew my big chance. The story begins in 1989, when the guy who was to make chess supercomputer Deep Blue for IBM was my graduate school officemate at Carnegie Mellon. His little side project was called Chiptest, and I would play the chess program all day long, to the dismay of my professors.

Although I was a U.S.-ranked chess master, Chiptest (and its successor, Deep Thought) destroyed me nearly every game. Then IBM bought the project, and I was left alone—that is, until the summer of 1991, when I was offered the chance to work on the Deep Blue project. I turned it down. "IBM?" I thought. "Don't they make those crappy PCs and mainframes?" I regretted my decision for years, particularly when in 1997 Deep Blue beat world champion Garry Kasparov.

When I thought PC, I thought IBM-PC, because my friends and I would play games on our IBMs. I knew two other things about the company: It was into mainframes and had been around forever. Also, it had something to do with typewriters way back when.

Now, in early 2008, IBM has more than $91 billion in revenues, $19 billion in cash flows, and nothing to do with PCs. In 2004 it sold its PC business to the China-based Lenovo Group for $1.75 billion. Lenovo became a PC powerhouse, its IBM blessing taking it to revenues of more than $12 billion, a fourfold increase.

So what does IBM do now? Where do the revenues come from, and, more important, is IBM cheap now because people on Wall Street have no clue what it actually does? A friend of mine who runs a long/short hedge fund said, "It's all about mainframes now, but it's slow-moving, low-margin growth."

Actually, only 24 percent of IBM's revenues come from mainframes. The rest is software and services. IBM's $48 billion services business has undergone dramatic changes, with more emphasis on higher-margin engagements. Its services division has had eight consecutive quarters of year-to-year improvement in gross profit. And those margins drove cash flows: $15.3 billion in 2006, compared with $14.4 billion for Microsoft and $11.4 billion for Hewlett-Packard—more than the cash flows for Dell, Oracle, and Accenture combined.

That has allowed the company to go on a mega buying spree since 2004, acquiring thirty-four software companies, all in high-growth niches. In 2006 alone, IBM invested $4.8 billion for fourteen acquisitions (eleven software, two services). Its investments in systems-management software companies, including the Micromuse acquisition, have contributed to the strong performance of Tivoli (revenues up 44 percent year over year in the third quarter of 2006 and 25 percent in the fourth quarter).

What has the company been doing with the rest of the money? Giving it back to shareholders and quietly taking itself private. Since January 2003, IBM has returned $32.4 billion to shareholders ($27.2 billion through share buybacks and $5.2 billion in dividends). In 2007 it bought back more than 1.2 billion shares. Companies often do this, and it usually doesn't reduce their share count because they issue options to employees, use stock to make acquisitions, issue convertible debt, and take other dilutive measures. But in IBM's case, share count has gone down every year since 2003, when it had 1.73 billion. It now has 1.553 billion shares, a reduction of 10 percent. Again, it's slowly taking itself private. This has the effect of increasing earnings per share and creating an imbalance in the supply versus demand equation for the shares.

In terms of the low-margin business, it is worth comparing IBM to its closest competitors, in particular Hewlett-Packard. In fiscal 2006, IBM had $91.4 billion in revenues while H-P had slightly more at $91.7 billion. Pretax income for IBM was $13.3 billion; for H-P, $7.2 billion. IBM's overall net income margin was 13.2 percent compared with H-P's 6.7 percent. Not bad.

I also like the fact that IBM is included in the Ocean Tomo 300 Patent Index (see chapter 18), an equity index derived from the value of corporate intellectual property. It is based on academic research showing that companies that spend money on research and development tend to outperform broader indices. Wall Street analysts count R & D as expenses, but it adds to the intangible book value of a company. In other words, the typical analyst looks at R & D as a negative, even though in the long term it pays off.

IBM received 3,621 patents last year, bringing the total to more than 40,000. No other company has ever received even 3,000 patents in a year. It attained more patents last year than Google, Dell, Apple, Microsoft, General Electric, and EMC Corporation combined.

Although IBM is known as a mainframe company, a big portion of its research is focused on building nanotube transistors. Commercialization is years away, but when it happens, people might forget completely that IBM had something to do with typewriters back in the day.

Next on the list is Disney (DIS). The media group has made the news this past year for its multibillion-dollar merger with the animation company Pixar, but more important is the firm's domination of television and music over the past year.

While I was writing this, I looked at the cable TV rankings: Three of the top ten shows were repeats of the Disney Channel original film *Jump In*. Top was the original showing, followed by *Cory in the House*, which came on right before *Jump In*.

Meanwhile, the *Jump In* album was a top seller, and the sound-track, based on the Disney Channel hit for 2006, *High School Musical*, was the number-one selling album in 2007. Disney is on fire with the teen demographic. It has the formula down, and we will continue to see the numbers proving it.

In terms of share repurchases, the company bought back 243 million shares of stock in 2006 for about $6.9 billion. In 2005, Disney bought back 91 million shares for $2.4 billion. The company has authorization to buy back an additional 206 million shares. It has also committed to buying back enough shares to keep its number of shares outstanding equal to the total before the Pixar takeover, which was purchased for stock.

The health-care benefits company Cigna (CI) is another one that is regularly out there buying back its shares. Like IBM, I would argue that it is slowly taking itself private. The company repurchased approximately 8.4 million shares for $931 million during the third quarter of 2006 and about 22.6 million shares for $2.4 billion (or $106.19 a share) year-to-date through October 2007. Shares outstanding have gone from 140 million at the end of 2002 to 112 million at the end of 2006. Consequently, its price-to-equity ratio keeps getting lower as earnings rise and the number of shares shrinks. It's currently trading for just 12 times its forward cash flows. Carl Icahn is a shareholder of the company, as is value investor David Dreman, and my guess is that at some point this will either be a leveraged buyout or an activist investor situation.

My takeaway from this is that, no matter how many academic degrees someone has, try not to listen too much to them. Common sense suggests that in any market when you reduce supply but demand remains the same, the underlying asset goes up. Throw in the fact that more cash is produced to reduce supply further, and you have an excellent bullish scenario.

Finally, one of my favorite stocks for a forever portfolio combines three of the attributes discussed here and in chapter 18 on patents:

- The company is aggressively repurchasing its shares.
- The company has strong patent protection.
- The company surfs on top of perhaps the strongest demographic trend mentioned in this book—the tendency for human beings to get lazier every year.

Universal Electronics (UEIC) licenses all the patents for the remote controls for your TV and other home entertainment devices. The company is repurchasing shares every year and consistently growing revenues by 10–20 percent each year. With the patent protection behind it and the tendency for people to sit on their backsides watching TV most of the time, this company is a perfect addition to the forever portfolio.

It's important to remember that I'm not necessarily recommending these stocks for the short term. Rather, I'm pointing out they're the type of companies that over the long term are slowly taking their shares over the market and thereby increasing value for a forever portfolio.

Bubble 2.0

WOMEN'S LEGS AND TATTOOS

Every time that I look in the mirror
All these lines on my face gettin' clearer.
—Aerosmith

L et's forget about the Internet for a bit. In Silicon Valley, there's a popular bumper sticker that reads, PLEASE GOD, LET THERE BE ANOTHER BUBBLE. If the Internet was a bubble again, everyone there would get back on track toward making billions. That's fine, best of luck to them. But we have other things to focus on.

So what's next? Clearly, the World Wide Web (as opposed to certain stocks) did not prove to be the bubble it was widely accused of being. Instead we have a demographic trend of rising Internet use around the world that's still only on first base or in the first inning or the first quarter, or whatever other analogy you want to use. There's only one more demographic trend I can think of that's almost as explosive in terms of the potential for profit: Of course, I'm talking about increased concern for the care and maintenance of women's legs.

Source: Matthew Bowden, www.digitallyrefreshing.com, via Wikipedia Commons.

A combination of three trends—the post–World War II Baby Boom, increased life expectancies, and the shrinking workweek (resulting in more leisure time)—mean that women aged 45–55 increasingly are looking to medical solutions for cosmetic problems in skin care and rejuvenation, varicose veins, and weight issues. With a million more people each year entering that demographic than leaving it, the companies that service this group are not as subject to economic pressures as, say, General Motors (GM) or Wal-Mart (WMT), which live or die on the basis of every uptick or downtick in consumer spending. Two companies, in particular, have the cash, the current investor base, and the technology to be worth looking at for a forever portfolio.

Venus Medical Technologies (VNUS) specializes in noninvasive outpatient treatment of varicose veins. About 25 million people in the United States and another 40 million in Western Europe suffer from varicose veins. In 2006 alone, 1.2 million sought treatment for the condition. The reason so few seek treatment (in relation to the total number with the malady) is that it often involves painful, invasive surgery (removing the vein in question) with many potential side effects. The Venus procedure, in contrast, is to give the patient a radio frequency (RF) generator, which provides the power and monitoring for a disposable catheter that heats the vein. The disposable catheters generate recurring revenues for the company. Out of the market of 65 million people with varicose vein conditions, only about sixty thousand have used the company's method for treatment. Revenues have gone up every year since Venus first started selling its product in 1999, and the company has been profitable since the fourth quarter of 2003.

Syneron Medical (ELOS) is another strong player in this sector. This company also uses RF energy to deliver heat to the layers of the skin below the epidermis, avoiding the burning associated with other skin treatments. With Syneron's device, doctors can constantly monitor the level of heat and energy they are applying to an area and adjust the instrument accordingly. Its treatments have been used for wrinkles, leg veins, acne, cellulite, and a host of other cosmetic problems. Revenue and income for the company have gone up every year since 2001.

The shrinking workweek is part of the reason why demand for aesthetic and cosmetic procedures is up. People simply have more time on their hands to socialize. Every month, it seems, economists go into spasms over each fractional change in the average workweek. The perception is that if people work fewer hours, the economy is going into a death spiral. In 1900, the average workweek was more than sixty hours. People (including children) regularly worked twelve-hour days, five days a week.

Perhaps we should've all started shorting the market when the average workweek went down to fifty-nine hours. Now, depending on your source of economic statistics, the average workweek is somewhere between thirty-five and forty hours. For the extreme outlier, visit the National Sleep Foundation, which says the average workweek is forty-six hours—but that doesn't include coffee breaks.

AND LET'S NOT FORGET ABOUT TATTOOS

I thank God I never got drunk enough to get a tattoo, and apparently I'm not alone. Six million Americans who have tattoos want to get rid of them. According to the Sunday *New York Times*, 45 million Americans have gotten tattoos, and 17 percent of them regret it. By comparison, *Life* magazine estimated in 1936 that only 10 million Americans had tattoos. And the problem is only going to grow. More people are getting tattoos than ever, which means that in the coming decades, more people will be wanting to remove their tattoos than ever.

When someone gets a tattoo, hundreds of pinpoint needle pricks are made in the skin, and each one is filled with pigment. To remove the tattoo, a pinpoint laser is aimed into each hole to disintegrate the pigment cells. The treatments are painful and expensive. The laser process can take anywhere from six to twenty separate treatments. According to the *Times* story, each treatment is like thousands of rubber bands snapping against your skin. Still, as Baby Boomers age, what was once a daring picture of Satan on their right shoulder is now just a flabby red grinning face, laughing at them. Clearly, this is a trend we can invest in.

Companies that specialize in tattoo removal aren't only focused on tattoos; fortunately for us, they tend to specialize in the larger demographic trend of using lasers for aesthetic treatments and cosmetic procedures like wrinkle and scar removal, and skin tightening. These procedures are growing industrywide at a pace of 30 percent per year.

The stock in this sector that I think especially deserves inclusion in a forever portfolio is Cynosure (CYNO). Cynosure develops and uses lasers for aesthetic treatment—everything from cellulite removal to varicose-vein removal (see below) to tattoo removal. Here are some before and after shots from its Web site:

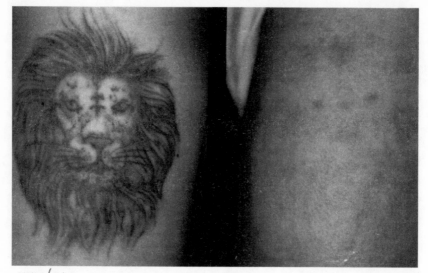

CYNOSURE   Courtesy of Henrik Mikkelsen, MD

Other companies that take advantage of the twin trends involving women's legs and minimally invasive cosmetic procedures include Cutera (CUTR), which manufactures laser aesthetic systems for hair removal, leg vein removal, and skin rejuvenation. Vascular Solutions (VASC) is a medical-device manufacturer that markets the Vari-Lase endovenous laser, which is used for the treatment of varicose veins. Iridex (IRIX) is a provider of therapeutic laser systems for dermatological and eye conditions. It has laser systems for various aesthetic treatments, such as hair and leg vein removal and sun-damage treatment.

As a play on the completely noninvasive side, what about covering those women's legs up? We can't ignore companies such as Hanesbrands (HSI), which manufactures hosiery under the brands Hanes, L'eggs, and Just My Size. Although it's a smaller part of its business, Limited Brands' (LTD) Victoria's Secret division does make stockings. And finally, Frederick's of Hollywood (FOH) owns women's clothing stores that sell stockings and other intimate apparel.

7

Crime and Punishment

I wish the following two charts were the price charts of stocks I own:

STATE PRISON POPULATION BY OFFENSE TYPE, 1980-2004

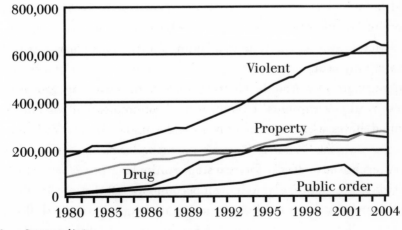

Source: Department of Justice

JAIL POPULATIONS BY AGE AND GENDER, 1990–2006

Number of jail inmates (one-day count)

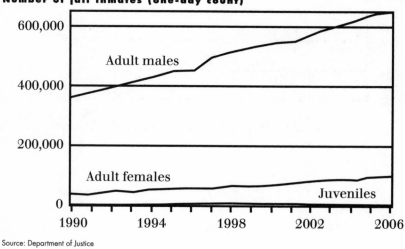

Source: Department of Justice

In addition, the number of people on parole has gone up every year for the past forty years—an average of 2.2 percent per year. Crime is increasing, and not only in the United States, but worldwide. Guess what will happen in all developing countries as more people move from rural areas to urban areas: More crimes will happen, more people will get caught, and more prisons will get filled.

Here's another nice little graph (see figure on page 67).

Two takeaways: Everyone is spending more money year over year on not only crime prevention but also the incarceration process, including court fees. And the federal government is pushing these costs on to local governments. This suggests three trends that will hit the United States, and then spread worldwide:

1. Alternatives to deadly force to stop criminals.
2. Crime prevention before it even becomes an issue.
3. Private prisons, as local governments no longer have the skill sets to handle the increase in need for professional facilities.

DIRECT EXPENDITURE BY LEVEL OF GOVERNMENT, 1982-2005

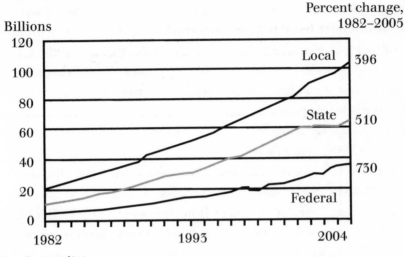

Source: Department of Justice

Taser International (TASR)® manufactures product lines for law enforcement and the prison corrections market, which include the Advanced Taser® M26™ and the Taser® X26™. The stock has a P/E of 50.

The Advanced Taser® M26™

The TASER was invented in order to give law-enforcement offi-
cers an alternative to a conventional firearm when extreme force is
needed to restrain or apprehend a criminal. It handles much like a
paintball gun but fires two dartlike electrodes that shock the target
into submission. There's a lot of controversy over whether the
TASER has actually been successful in lowering the number of
deaths caused by police trying to catch a suspect, but suffice it to say,
it's the best alternative now. And if I were a criminal, I'd rather be
shot by a TASER than a gun.

Perhaps best known for the hands-free Roomba vacuum, iRobot
Corp. (IRBT) also makes robotic products for the law-enforcement
and Homeland Security markets. It manufactures the PackBot EOD,
which is a strong, lightweight robot built to conduct explosives and
hazardous materials disposal, as well as do search and surveillance
for bomb squads and SWAT teams.

The crime boom will also benefit Brinks Co. (BCO). Brinks is in
the business of transportation and cash-logistics services, but also
provides electronic security systems for single-family residences,
commercial properties, and multifamily housing. The trend will also
expand the private-prisons industry. Michael Brush of MSN Money
gives three reasons why growth in private prison companies is here
to stay:

- **"Increased border patrols."** Basically, the Intelligence Reform
  and Terrorism Prevention Act of 2004 increased the border patrols that will crack down on illegal immigration. According to
  President Bush, lawmakers estimate that by 2010 another 40,000
  prison beds will be needed for those illegal immigrants who are
  caught.
- **"Governments are hard up for cash."** According to Brush, local and federal governments are cutting their prison construction budgets by 48 percent. Instead, governments are turning to
  the private sector in part because costs are up to 10 to 15 percent
  lower.

- **"Government prisons are overcrowded and the prison population will keep growing."** According to Brush, the private sector is being asked to meet the increasing demands of a prison system that is already at overcapacity in over half the states.

Demand should pick up over the next decade for a simple demographic reason. The children of Baby Boomers, the so-called Echo Boom, are about to enter the eighteen- to twenty-four-year-old age group—the years when people commit the most crimes. The Federal Bureau of Prisons estimates it will have a 36,000-bed shortfall by 2010, partly due to this trend.

For your forever portfolio, here are a few primary beneficiaries from this rising trend over the next fifty years. The largest private prison system in both market cap and revenues is Corrections Corp. of America (CXW), which is a Nashville-based company with more than forty facilities. The second-largest prison company is Geo Group, Inc. (GEO), based in Boca Raton, Florida. It maintains facilities in the United States, Australia, Canada, South Africa, and the United Kingdom. Cornell Companies, Inc. (CRN), is a Houston, Texas, prison company, which in addition to providing detention services, also offers educational services to detainees.

THE IDENTITY-THEFT INDEX

Late in 2007 I got the call that I had been most dreading: "Mr. Altucher, we believe there has been unauthorized use of your credit card." Not only that, they were calling about a Visa card that I had no recollection of owning, and about a string of purchases made during September 2005, although they wouldn't tell me what those purchases were. I don't own a Visa. I've owned nothing but American Express cards forever. Damn! My identity had been stolen!

It had never happened to me before, so I started looking into it. The Federal Trade Commission (FTC) reports that it received

250,000 complaints about identity theft in 2005. Credit card fraud, at 26 percent of total complaints, was the most common form of reported identity theft. Phone or utilities fraud came in next at 18 percent, bank fraud at 17 percent, and employment fraud at 12 percent. Government benefits fraud, at 9 percent, and loan fraud, at 5 percent, were the least common.

Depending on the type of theft, the average consumer takes up to three hundred hours of time to resolve an identity theft situation. Also, many cases of identity theft are not discovered until up to eighteen months after the event happened. There are several ways to play off this growing trend, especially with companies that create software for credit card providers to monitor potential identity theft situations.

I like the sector because this is a problem that's never going away—and the rise of the Internet has made it easier than ever for thieves to snag credit card numbers online and pose as another person, because the transaction interface is much more impersonal than a phone or face-to-face purchase. In fact, reported fraud complaints to the FTC have gone from 542,000 in 2003 to 686,000 in 2005, and I'm sure many situations are unreported or not even discovered yet. In addition, the sector is largely unknown from a stock-analyst perspective, and many of these companies tend to be underfollowed. And finally, from a forever portfolio perspective, these companies are not going to be affected at all by the economy. Identity theft is here to stay, and all the companies mentioned below are going to be in business for a long time.

Intersections, Inc. (INTX), has the software to do monitoring for unusual activity on credit cards. It also offers identity theft insurance, fraud recovery assistance, preemployment background screening, reference checks, and drug testing. Almost all of its revenues come from its identity theft software and services. This could change at any time, but many great value investors have backed up the truck on INTX, including Royce, Heartland, and Renaissance Technologies.

Equifax (EFX) collects, organizes, and manages various types of financial, demographic, and marketing information. Its products and services are categorized as follows: information services, marketing services, and personal solutions. Relevant to our portfolio is this last division, which has services to provide information to consumers enabling them to reduce their exposure to identity fraud and to better manage their credit health.

ChoicePoint (CPS) provides information products and services to Fortune 1000 corporations, consumer finance companies, asset-based lenders, legal and professional service providers, health-care service providers, nonprofit organizations, small businesses, and consumers. Major offerings include DNA identification services, background screenings, drug-testing administration services, public filing searches, credential verification, authentication services, visual investigative and link-analysis software, data visualization, analytics, and data-integration services.

So what happened with my identity theft call? It turns out it was an Amazon.com Visa that one James Altucher signed up for in September, used to buy some books (including an order of my last book, *SuperCash*), and then promptly forgot about. Now I need to find out what stocks are good for memory enhancement (see chapter 9) so I don't waste three hours on hold with the credit card company again.

8

The Forever Diet

L et's forget about stocks for a second. Stocks lead to worry, and that leads to ill health and misery. Not to mention, it's pointless to worry about concepts that I view as rather esoteric relative to the concept of making money—concepts like the current-account deficit or an inverted yield curve. The inverted yield curve is a predictor of nothing, and the current-account deficit is most likely a sign that good times are coming—just look at the countries with surpluses throughout recent history, such as Japan and Germany in the 1990s.

Let's worry instead about my waistline. I'd like to lose weight. Why? Well, for one thing, if you want to live forever, there's evidence that monitoring caloric intake can add years to your life. Well, at least if you're a mouse or a spider. From Wikipedia: "In 1986, [Richard] Weindruch reported that restricting the calorie intake of laboratory mice proportionally increased their lifespan compared to a group of mice with a normal diet. The calorie-restricted mice also maintained youthful appearances and activity levels longer, and showed delays in age-related diseases."

Basically, restricting calories while maintaining all other nutrient levels helps to reduce cholesterol and blood pressure. Aging usually results in increases in both, leading to various diseases that eventually cause death. Also, other studies have shown that intermittent fasting has slowed the progress of Alzheimer's and Parkinson's diseases. Again, from Wikipedia:

> Studies by Mark P. Mattson, Ph.D., chief of the National Institute on Aging's (NIA) Laboratory of Neurosciences, and colleagues have found that intermittent fasting and calorie restriction affect the progression of diseases similar to Huntington's disease, Parkinson's disease, and Alzheimer's disease in mice (PMID 11119686). In one study, rats and mice ate a low-calorie diet or were deprived of food for 24 hours every other day (PMID 12724520). Both methods improved glucose metabolism, increased insulin sensitivity, and increased stress resistance. Researchers have long been aware that calorie restriction extends lifespan, but this study showed that improved glucose metabolism also protects neurons in experimental models of Parkinson's and stroke.

So, aside from looking good, reducing calories somewhat is critical for maintaining a forever portfolio simply because it allows you to manage that portfolio a few years longer—if calorie restriction does, in fact, work for humans, which is still unclear.

But there are more reasons to want to lose weight. Most people are unhappy with their physical appearance and often feel their lives would be better and happier if they could just lose a few pounds. And the trend toward an increasing number of not only overweight people but also to morbidly obese people in the United States is one that will continue for the next fifty years, and there's nothing we can really do about it.

So let's not fight it. If you are a long-term investor or even an entrepreneur, the weight-loss industry represents fertile ground for making money over the next fifty years. The Baby Boomers and their children need you!

Baby Boomers are the first generation to be less healthy than their parents. They have spent more years living with more obesity than the previous generation. The numbers are simply shocking: Two-thirds of Americans are overweight or obese. One-third of Americans are obese, as defined as by their body-mass index, which I'll explain below. Approximately 60 million Americans are obese, and 9 million are severely obese. Within 50 years, obesity will likely shorten the average life span of 77.6 years by at least 2 to 5 years, more than the impact of cancer or heart disease. This trend could reverse the mostly steady increase in American life expectancy that has occurred in the past two centuries, and it will have tremendous social and economic consequences.

Since the mid-1970s in America, both adults and children have experienced a sharp increase in the odds of becoming obese or overweight. Among adults aged twenty to seventy-four, obesity's prevalence increased from 15 percent during the 1976–80 period, to 32.9 percent during the 2003–04 period. In terms of pounds, 3.8 million Americans are over 300 pounds, while 400,000 Americans (mostly men) weigh more than 400 pounds. The average adult woman in the United States weighs in at an all-time high of 163 pounds.

The prevalence of obesity among children has quadrupled over the past twenty-five years. Up to 30 percent of U.S. children are overweight, and childhood obesity has more than doubled in the past quarter century.

Furthermore, this overweight trend has steadily increased over the years in both sexes and all ages, races, ethnic groups, smoking levels, and even education levels. From 1960 to 2002, the percentage of overweight people increased by 20.4 percent to a total of 65.2 percent of U.S. adults aged twenty to seventy-four. The percentage of obese people more than doubled in the same age range, coming to a total of 30.5 percent. Most of this surge has occurred in the last twenty years. For instance, from 1988 to 2002, extreme obesity increased from 2.9 percent to 4.9 percent, compared to 0.8 percent in 1960.

MEASURING OBESITY

A number of methods are used to determine if someone is overweight or obese. Some are based on the relationship between height and weight; others are based on measurements of body fat. The method most commonly used today is body-mass index (BMI), which is weight adjusted for the height of an individual.

BMI can be used to screen for both overweight and obese adults. It is the measurement of choice for many obesity researchers and other health professionals, as well as the definition used in most published information on overweight and obesity. BMI does not directly measure percent of body fat, but it is a more accurate indicator of overweight and obesity than relying on weight alone. To determine BMI, multiply weight in pounds by 704.5, divide the result by height in inches, and then divide that result by height in inches a second time.

The medical community generally considers people with a BMI of 25 to 29.9 to be overweight, while obesity is defined as a BMI greater than 30. A BMI equal to or more than 35 indicates severe obesity.

BODY-MASS INDEX TABLE

To use the table, find the appropriate height in the left-hand column and
then move across to a given weight. The number at the top of the column
is the BMI at that height and weight. Pounds have been rounded off.

BMI	19	20	21	22	23	24	25	26	27	28
Height (inches)	Body Weight (pounds)									
58	91	96	100	105	110	115	119	124	129	134
59	94	99	104	109	114	119	124	128	133	138
60	97	102	107	112	118	123	128	133	138	143
61	100	106	111	116	122	127	132	137	143	148
62	104	109	115	120	126	131	136	142	147	153
63	107	113	118	124	130	135	141	146	152	158
64	110	116	122	128	134	140	145	151	157	163
65	114	120	126	132	138	144	150	156	162	168
66	118	124	130	136	142	148	155	161	167	173
67	121	127	134	140	146	153	159	166	172	178
68	125	131	138	144	151	158	161	171	177	184
69	128	135	142	149	155	162	169	176	182	189
70	132	139	146	153	160	167	174	181	188	195
71	136	143	150	157	165	172	179	186	193	200
72	140	147	154	162	169	177	184	191	199	206
73	144	151	159	166	147	182	189	197	204	212
74	148	155	163	171	179	186	194	202	210	218
75	152	160	166	176	184	192	200	208	216	224
76	156	164	172	180	189	197	205	213	221	230

29	30	31	32	33	34	35	36	37	38	39	40
Body Weight (pounds)											
138	143	148	153	158	162	167	172	177	181	186	191
143	148	153	158	163	168	173	178	183	188	193	198
148	153	158	163	168	174	179	184	189	194	199	204
153	158	164	169	174	180	185	190	195	201	206	211
158	164	169	175	180	186	191	196	202	207	213	218
163	169	175	180	186	191	197	203	208	214	220	225
169	174	180	186	192	197	204	209	215	221	227	232
174	180	186	192	198	204	210	216	222	228	234	240
179	186	192	198	204	210	216	223	229	235	241	247
185	191	198	204	211	217	223	230	236	242	249	255
190	197	204	210	216	223	230	236	243	249	256	262
196	203	210	216	223	230	236	243	250	257	263	270
202	209	216	222	229	236	243	250	257	264	271	278
208	215	222	229	236	243	250	257	265	272	279	286
213	221	228	235	242	250	258	265	272	279	287	294
219	227	235	242	250	257	265	272	280	288	295	302
225	233	242	249	256	264	272	280	287	295	303	311
232	240	248	256	264	272	279	287	295	303	311	319
238	246	265	263	271	279	287	295	304	312	320	328

MEDICAL CONDITIONS LINKED TO OBESITY

Obesity is putting Americans at risk for thirty-five major diseases, including dyslipidemia (high triglycerides or high cholesterol), coronary heart disease, stroke, type 2 diabetes, gallbladder disease, osteoarthritis, respiratory problems and sleep apnea (impaired breathing and oxygen deprivation during sleep), and various types of cancer, especially endometrial and colon cancer.

Furthermore, a study published in the September 2006 issue of the *American Journal of Public Health* showed more obesity-related arthritis among Baby Boomers compared to the previous generation. Arthritis risk soared along with the obesity rates of Baby Boomers, and arthritis cases attributed to obesity rose from 3 percent to 18 percent between 1971 and 2002. This rise can be attributed to multiple factors, including changes in the way physicians diagnose arthritis, but researchers say the rise in obesity cannot be ignored as a factor. "Baby-boomers are just approaching the age when arthritis rates begin to rise dramatically. Many baby-boomers have lived with obesity for much of their lives. We can expect to see the health and functional consequences of this epidemic in the coming decades," said the authors.

Medical risks for overweight and obese children and adolescents are significant as well. For instance, type 2 diabetes accounted for 2 to 4 percent of all childhood diabetes before 1992, but skyrocketed to 16 percent by 1994. Childhood diabetes overall has increased tenfold in the past twenty years. The parallel increase in the number of obese children and adolescents is reported to be one of the most significant factors for the rise in diabetes. Obese adolescents and children are reported to be a whopping 12.6 times more likely than nonobese adolescents and children to have high fasting blood insulin levels, a significant risk factor for type 2 diabetes.

Among obese children and adolescents, persistently elevated blood pressure levels, or hypertension, has been found to occur approximately nine times more frequently than in the nonobese. Another startling difference between obese and nonobese children and adolescents is that the obese are 4.5 times more likely to have high systolic blood pressure and 2.4 times more likely to have high diastolic blood pressure.

Orthopedic complications are also present in obese children and adolescents, as growing children's bones and cartilage are in the process of development and are not strong enough to bear excess weight. In younger children, excess weight can lead to bowing and overgrowth of leg bones. Increased weight on the growth plate of the hip can cause pain and limit range of motion, and 30 to 50 percent of children with this condition are overweight.

Sleep apnea occurs in about 7 percent of all children with obesity, and poor logical thinking skills are common in children with sleep apnea and obesity. In addition, there are the psychosocial effects and stigma for overweight children, leading to the potential development of negative body image and eating disorders.

THE COSTS OF OBESITY

A study of health-care expenditures directly related to overweight and obesity showed that they accounted for 9.1 percent of total U.S. medical costs in 1998, and could have gone as high as $78.5 billion ($92.6 billion in 2002 dollars). Medicaid and Medicare paid approximately 50 percent of these costs.

The estimated total cost of overweight and obesity in 2002 was $117 billion. The direct cost (medical spending) was $61 billion, while the indirect cost (lost productivity, disability payments, and the like) was $56 billion. According to the Social Security Administration, $77 million is paid monthly to approximately 137,000 persons who have met obesity requirements for disability.

In short, a ton of money is going to be spent for the next hundred years fighting this problem. But just as Sisyphus could never roll the boulder up the mountain, the task is never going to end.

AMERICANS AND EXERCISE

Only 26 percent of U.S. adults engage in vigorous leisure-time physical activity lasting ten minutes or more three or more times per week. About 59 percent of adults do no vigorous physical activity at all in their leisure time. For me, I like to walk. And here's an interesting little fact: One hundred laughs burns as many calories as about ten minutes of rowing. It's not always easy to laugh when you trade or invest for a living, but I try to make humor an important part of each day.

That said, it's still good to get up and exert yourself. People working in offices tend to be lazy most of the time. Drive to work, sit around staring at a computer, drive home, watch TV, sleep. Repeat.

About 25 percent of young people (ages twelve to twenty-one) participate in light-to-moderate activity (e.g., walking, bicycling) nearly every day. About 50 percent regularly engage in vigorous physical activity. Approximately 25 percent report no vigorous physical activity, and 14 percent report no recent vigorous or light-to-moderate physical activity. The direct cost of physical inactivity may be as high as $24.3 billion.

DEATHS FROM OBESITY

Individuals who are obese have a 10 to 50 percent increased risk of death compared with healthy-weight individuals; most of the increased risk is due to cardiovascular causes. Each year 300,000 premature deaths are associated with obesity. This translates into 25,000 per month, 5,769 per week, 821 per day, and 34 per hour. Of these deaths, 280,000 are adults.

Individuals with BMIs greater than 40 have death rates from cancer that are 52 percent higher for men and 62 percent higher for women than rates for their normal-weight counterparts. Obesity could account for 14 percent of cancer deaths among men and 20 percent among women in the United States. In both men and women, higher BMI is believed to translate into higher mortality rates from cancers of the colon and rectum, esophagus, liver, pancreas, gallbladder, and kidney. The same trend applies to cancers of the stomach and prostate in men and cancers of the breast, uterus, cervix, and ovaries in women. In one study, women gaining more than twenty pounds from age eighteen to midlife doubled their risk of breast cancer compared to those whose weight remained stable.

So how can we make money off of this? As usual, there's the front door and the backdoor to examine. The front door includes companies involved in dieting. In 1991, about 8,500 commercial diet centers were in operation across the country, many of them owned by a half dozen or so well-known national companies. Let's look at some of the more popular diets out there.

With a 2006 net income of $209 million—representing a one-year net-income jump of 21 percent—Weight Watchers (WTW) is one of the giants of the diet industry.

Founded in the 1960s by Jean Nidetch, Weight Watchers offers various products and services to assist with weight loss and maintenance. It started as a support group to help people lose weight and keep it off, and it now operates in about thirty countries around the world.

The program combines weight loss and exercise ideas. As a membership incentive, the company offers special foods, cookbooks, and exercise plans. Weight Watchers points are awarded for success, and the dieter has the support of Weight Watchers groups around the world and chapter members from his or her local group. The advantages are that one can lose weight with the support of others who are fighting the same battles, and that the Weight Watchers products are readily available.

NutriSystem (NTRI) offers its clients prepackaged meals every day, as well as books and other products related to its weight-loss initiatives. The company is phenomenally profitable, with a 75 percent return on equity and 200 percent year-over-year growth in earnings.

It also has $80 million in the bank and no debt. While it may not continue to grow at 200 percent per year, it's a safe bet that it will remain strong.

Right now NutriSystem is targeting the ever-increasing trend of men going on diet programs. In the February 2007 issue of *Barron's*, Ken Mertz, who runs the Forward Emerald Growth Fund, had this to say about NTRI: "I think their main growth driver that we see in 2007 continues to be the expansion of the men's line. They do a lot of advertising with ex-athletes, especially football players, drawing in men. Then they are also introducing this year the senior's program. Most of the advertising and programs, from Weight Watchers to Jenny Craig and so on, have been more geared to the female side."

THE FOREVER PORTFOLIO DIET

People swear by their diets, then they go off their diets. Then they feel guilty, and go back on. Do diets work? Not really. About 80 percent of people who go on diets leave them within five weeks. One year later, on average, people are back up to their prediet weight or higher. This raises an ethical issue: It's one thing to invest in a rising trend, such as Americans using diets to battle increasing obesity. It's another thing to invest in a trendy solution that's actually ineffective. Diet companies may not really help most of their clients, but they can be said to satisfy people's craving—particularly every new year—to do something about a part of their lives they find dissatisfying.

I prefer to always err on the side of making money. True, diets don't tend to work. But it's not the diet's fault, it's that people lack discipline. Because of the rising standard of living in the United States (which, in general, is a very good thing), it's as if people were living in a permanent college-freshman state. You're away from home for the first time, you have some money from your parents (or from a job for the first time in your life), and everything goes, particularly your waistline as you gain those "freshman fifteen" pounds.

Well, now that feeling of freedom you get when you enter college is permanent. The quality of life for Americans is going to continue to improve. The middle class is shrinking, not because people are getting poorer but because members of the middle class are improving their financial status and joining the upper classes, thanks to increased asset value, improving career prospects, better entrepreneurial opportunities, and the general prosperity of the country we live in.

Do some diets work better than others? There have been no conclusive studies on this, but my guess is that all diets *can* work. Any discipline at all in this area of life will pay great dividends. I'll tell you my own experience: When I lived in Manhattan, I always was able to keep my weight down because I walked everywhere. If I had to go to a meeting thirty blocks away (about a mile and a half), I would walk. In the middle of the winter in 2002, I moved up the Hudson River to a small town. I stopped walking completely; I'd go out for big breakfasts every morning and then I would work at home for the rest of the day. Within three months, I gained about twenty pounds. So I decided to make up my own diet to prove that any discipline at all pays dividends. Here it is:

- Only one item for breakfast, and it doesn't matter which item. So, for instance, instead of eating a dish of eggs, potatoes, and bacon, I would eat a corn muffin, or a donut, or a side of bacon—and nothing else.
- No snacking. When people are on diets, they don't snack. When they go off diets, they snack. All snacks are bad if you want to reduce weight or not gain weight.
- Eat whatever you want for lunch. I'd go have steak and french fries.
- No white at night. I'd avoid pasta for dinner and apple pie for

dessert. I didn't want to completely eliminate carbs or sugar, but I figured I could eat those at lunch. For dinner I'd eat a steak, fish, vegetables, whatever.

Within about two months, I lost the twenty pounds. I didn't feel I was depriving myself, and I've more or less kept that diet since then. (However, I do have a weakness for the contents of hotel minibars.)

DO DRUGS WORK?

Another way to invest in the front door of the obesity trend is through the lucrative weight-loss-drug industry. But the dangers here include perilous medical side effects that may make these drugs more harmful than good. The most notable example is the heart damage caused by the late-nineties drug Phen-Fen, a combination of phentermine and fenfluramine. Phen-Fen was yanked from the market after a surge of lawsuits filed by patients who'd taken it and subsequently developed serious cardiac conditions.

Currently only three prescription drugs are on the market for weight loss: phentermine, Xenical (orlistat), sold by Roche and GlaxoSmithKline (GSK), and Meridia (sibutramine), sold by Abbott Laboratories (ABT). Obesity experts say these drugs are only moderately useful. All of them have potential side effects and probably work best in combination with a low-calorie diet. Meridia works on brain chemistry to make users feel full more quickly, and Xenical blocks absorption of fat into the intestines. People on Meridia typically lose no more than ten to fourteen pounds in a six-month interval, and those on Xenical lose even less, thirteen pounds in a year. Phentermine, an appetite suppressant, is only approved for short-term use, and even then, most people lose less than a pound a week. Often, as soon as people stop taking the drugs, their weight jumps right back up.

GlaxoSmithKline recently introduced Alli, a 60mg version of orlistat (Xenical is in 120mg capsules). Alli was approved by the FDA in February 2007 and debuted at the end of June 2007. It is available over the counter and costs about $50 for a month's supply (60 capsules). It is wildly popular, and initial supplies sold out quickly, no doubt bolstered by a heavy marketing campaign including TV spots and print ads. Consumers seem to be unfazed by the product's side effects, which include oily discharge and reduced bowel control (pharmacists have nicknamed the drug "butter butt").

Sympathomimetics are approved for short-term use, but can raise your blood pressure. These comprise a number of products, including phentermine (Lonamin, Oby-Cap, Adipex, and Fastin), mazindol (Sanorex and Mazanor), diethylpropion (Tenuate), phendimetrazine (Bontril, Melfiat, Adipost, Prelu-2, Statobex, and Plegine), and benzphetamine (Didrex). All of these can help you start your diet, but the side effects can be severe, from increased blood pressure and heart rate to physical dependence.

In addition, researchers have recently been studying weight loss for people taking the drugs Topamax and Zonegran, both of which are used to treat migraines and epilepsy. These drugs' unexpected side effect was discovered when people taking them noticed they were losing weight without trying. It's not completely understood how these drugs make people lose weight. It's been observed that they work on brain circuits controlling hunger, cravings, and satiety. Patients using them are less hungry and fill up faster, and they also lose the urge to gorge on calorie-laden snacks. People taking these drugs have lost an average of 6 to 10 percent of body weight.

Other front-door investing methods include weight-loss companies like Herbalife (HLF), which sells a variety of diet products, healthy snacks, and nutritional supplements. The company trades at just 9 times cash flows despite solid 40 percent year-over-year earnings growth, both for 2007 and expected for 2008. Of course, when I refer to 9 times cash flows, I'm quite aware that after this book comes out, or ten years from now, it won't always be at those levels. But these are the type of indicators I'm looking at now because companies like Herbalife are about to enter into a significant (heck, fifty-year) period of growth and expansion as these trends take hold in full force.

A mutual fund that I like to follow, which happens to own both Herbalife and NutriSystem, is the Winslow Green Growth Fund (WGGXF). It has beaten the S&P 500 by 6 percent per year for the past five years. It attempts environmentally responsible investing, which has proven quite successful since the fund's inception. Again, I like to piggyback the ideas of people smarter and more experienced than I am. All these guys have done since 1983 is try to beat the market by researching "clean" companies. So if this fund likes the weight-loss companies, they are certainly worth a look. The Winslow Green Growth Fund also owns Green Mountain Coffee Roasters (GMCR), which is another company worth looking at, particularly if you, like me, drink five or more cups of coffee a day and are not particularly fond of Starbucks.

Other front-door plays include fitness companies, such as Lifetime Fitness (LTM). Everyone's always impressed with the earnings and revenue growth of a company like Google, but physical fitness is perhaps the biggest growth industry there is. Everyone wants to join a gym when New Year's rolls around. You feel like you're accomplishing something, and you work out once or twice. And then reality sets in. The workload for the year gets heavier; the kids' after-school activities cut into your free time. But still, you have that gym membership for the year—and the company gets paid even if the gym remains empty.

Here's the growth of LTM revenues since it went public:

Year Ending	Revenue (millions)
12/06	$500.39
12/05	$381.04
12/04	$300.08
12/03	$246.43
12/02	$188.96
12/01	$133.43
12/00	$93.07
12/99	$54.26

Not so bad for a non-dot-com company. Note that in 2001 revenues were up 45 percent. Remember 2001?—recession, bear market, 9/11 attack, dot-com bust. But so what? People still felt the urge to lose weight.

THE BACKDOOR

Attacking the obesity trend head-on involves investing in companies that directly attempt to help people lower their weight. However, given all the side effects of obesity (sleep apnea, diabetes, arthritis), I also like to look at the companies that directly cater to those peripheral obesity markets.

But first, let's examine the surgical procedure that is probably the most successful for combating morbid obesity: gastric bypass surgery. In addition, some of the surgical products used in this procedure will have continual backdoor success in the expanding obesity trend.

In 1998, there were a total of 13,386 bariatric (obesity) surgeries performed. By 2002, the number had risen to 80,000. In 2003, this figure rose to 121,055 procedures. Severely obese people who undergo weight-loss surgery typically lose about forty-five to sixty-five pounds and maintain their lower weight for ten years or longer, according to the *Annals of Internal Medicine*. The vast majority of surgeries (85 percent) are performed on people between the ages of fifty-five and sixty-four, and bariatric surgery is far more common among women than men, with 82 percent female patients.

Roughly one-fifth of those who have weight-loss surgery experience complications, such as intestinal leaks, which can lead to additional operations and a longer hospitalization. The death rate from bariatric procedures is less than 1 percent.

Among patients who undergo bariatric surgery, 94 percent choose the gastric bypass procedure. These patients lose roughly twenty pounds more than those who undergo vertical-banded gastroplasty. A gastric bypass involves shrinking the stomach and altering the intestines to reduce the amount of calories and nutrients the body can absorb. According to two organizations, the American Society for Bariatric Surgery and the National Institutes of Health, Roux-en-Y gastric bypass surgery is the most popular bariatric surgery in the United States, and 83.7 percent of type 2 diabetes cases are resolved as a side result of the procedure. In vertical-banded gastroplasty, a band and staples are used to reduce stomach capacity and thus food intake.

In 1998, the overall hospital costs for bariatric surgery amounted to $147 million; by 2004, this figure had risen to $1.3 billion. In 2004, approximately 78 percent of the surgeries were paid for by private insurance, 7 percent were funded by Medicare, and 5 percent were funded by Medicaid. Only 5 percent were uninsured, laying to rest the myth that it's virtually impossible for an insurance company to cover the cost of gastric bypass surgery.

So how do we take advantage of the growth in bariatric surgery? Well, when the stomach is stapled back up, doctors need to use products for staple-line reinforcement, in order to prevent bleeding and allow time for the procedure to be completed. One reinforcement product that's had successful growth in this procedure is Peri-Strips, which are manufactured by Synovis Life Technologies (SYNO). Sales of Peri-Strips have been averaging 40 percent annual growth, with most of that fueled by the increase in gastric bypass surgery.

MY BREATHTAKING EXPERIENCE AS A RESPIRATORY THERAPIST

In 1993, I was a respiratory therapist in the ER and ICU floors of a major hospital in Cleveland. I had no training whatsoever, nor had I ever been in a hospital before. My tenure as a medical professional lasted one week. At the time I had just been asked to leave the graduate program in computer science at Carnegie Mellon University. (They said I could come back when I was "more mature," and I still have not gone back.) I was working as a computer programmer at CMU, and I got a call out of the blue from a doctor at the above-mentioned hospital. He was the father of my girlfriend's sister's boyfriend, and he had heard that I liked to write. He felt that the entire medical industry was too motivated by greed and, disgusted by it, wanted to reveal all but not use his name. So he wanted me to write a medical thriller based on his own experiences. He was a well-known heart surgeon, and he had a sense of urgency about the whole project because he had just been diagnosed with a very rare blood disease and had somewhere between six and twelve months to live.

So I went to his hospital for a week, staying at a Holiday Inn right outside of Cleveland, and he gave me a white coat and a little security badge and introduced me around as a visiting respiratory therapist. Oddly, nobody ever asked any hard questions, which was good, as I was only vaguely aware that *respiratory* had something to do with breathing. I would walk with other respiratory therapists on their rounds, doing nothing life threatening to any patients but just observing how the whole system works. I got a quick education on what to do if your top priority is to save your life: Never, ever get checked in to a hospital. The stories I would hear and even see in just that one week were beyond abhorrent, and I'm afraid to mention them here.

When I got back from my rounds, I started work on the book. But the doctor had a very specific plot in mind for the novel, which involved the character based on him having a torrid affair with a character based on another respiratory therapist who worked at the hospital. I didn't really want to do it that way, and for the first time ever I got a psychosomatic disease: I had carpal tunnel syndrome, and I couldn't type a single word for months. I went to doctors and chiropractors, and nothing worked. Four months later, my friend the doctor died of his blood disease. After that, I was able to write again and didn't suffer from carpal tunnel again for another four years, at which point acupuncture worked and seemed to cure me forever (eleven years and counting).

All of this is to say that life is to be lived as if it were an unfinished painting on a huge canvas. My doctor friend ultimately shed his body, unhappy with his life's work and not satisfied in his efforts (through me, unfortunately) to bring some light into it. As for me, I was able to experience a side of life I had never dreamed of experiencing. I learned something new and I was able to bring those new ideas into other disciplines. I was a computer programmer who wanted to be a writer, who became a respiratory therapist for a week, on the way toward all the other things I've done so far. I've just turned forty, and I hope the next forty years will bring equally interesting experiences into my life if I seek them out, keep my body healthy, and keep my mind open to these experiences.

From my vast experience as a respiratory therapist (see sidebar), I can say this with confidence: Everybody needs to breathe. And also, everyone needs to sleep. Here I'll discuss a company that helps with both.

As mentioned above, a common side effect of obesity is sleep apnea. Prior to gastric bypass surgery, patients must be screened for sleep apnea, because it could result in disaster due to breathing complications during and after the operation. ResMed (RMD) makes products to help people with any sort of breathing disorders that occur in sleep. As you can see from the chart (see the chart on p. 91), the sleep-apnea trend has been anything but sleepy.

RESMED INC.

as of Apr. 23, 2008

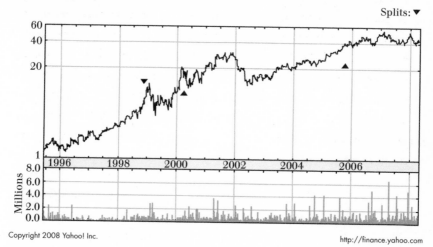

Splits: ▼

Copyright 2008 Yahoo! Inc.

http://finance.yahoo.com

There are opportunities to invest after gastric bypass surgery, too. Due to the popularity of the procedure, plastic surgeons are receiving an influx of patients who want to reshape their body after all that weight loss. More than 52,000 contouring procedures were performed for weight-loss patients in 2003. In the same year, the number of patients receiving buttocks lifts grew by 74 percent. The number of upper-arm lifts rose by 66 percent; lower-body lifts, 14 percent; and thigh lifts, 33 percent. In the past three years, the popularity of upper-arm lifts has seen tremendous growth, with a 1,938 percent increase; that of lower-body lifts has been even more extreme, with a 2,400 percent increase. Nearly 70 percent of the upper-arm and thigh lifts were performed on postbariatric patients. Some other common procedures performed after bariatric surgery are breast lifts, tummy tucks, and breast reductions.

The American Society of Plastic Surgeons projected that the number of body-contouring procedures performed on postbariatric patients would increase by at least 36 percent in 2004, based on a prediction by the American Society for Bariatric Surgery (ASBS) that more than 144,000 patients would have bariatric operations in

2004. (The actual number was about 121,000.) In 2003, more than 103,000 people went under the knife for gastric bypass surgery, compared with 67,000 people who did so in 2002, according to the ASBS.

Mentor (MNT) is a public company that is a leader in delivering body-contouring procedures. It has been a good long-term bet: A 2,000 percent return in twenty years? Not too shabby.

MENTOR CORP.
as of Apr. 23, 2008

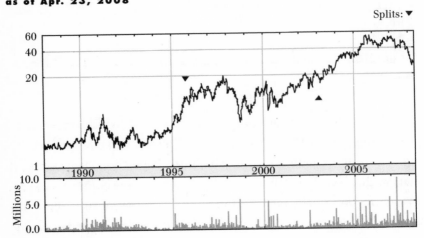

Splits: ▼

9

There's No Known Cure

P lease, please let me find out that I'm really an alien from outer space who was put in the body of a human with the standing mission to "observe, report, judge." At some point, fifty years out, the spaceship will come (I'm picturing the ship from the series premiere of *The Greatest American Hero*), they'll beam me up, and my memories will be restored to me. It will turn out that I'm immortal and my interstellar wife has been in suspended animation for ninety years while I was on my mission to Earth. Is it so unreasonable to have this fantasy? To find out there's a reason everything happened the way it did? That those moments when I was most introspective it was simply because I was processing the data of an incredibly complicated alien mission? Because, when the judgment is finally given, in the bowels of some intergalactic bureaucratic court, with the fate of the human race ("To the Phantom Zone? Or not?") in my hands, my judgment will be this: Humans are arrogant and, as a whole, they probably live too long.

At any rate, we certainly live longer than the seven gods of

Ragnarök originally intended in their blueprint for the moderately furry biped we were supposed to evolve into. Thirty years, tops, was supposed to be our life span. We did several things to disrupt this. We stopped killing each other as much, although we still do a lot of it. We started bathing regularly—well, present company excluded, but I'm grateful for everyone around me keeping clean. And we came up with various medicines that, at the very least, reduce symptoms, so we could be happier going about our day, and, at best, eliminated some pretty severe diseases that had been killing thirty- and forty-year-olds for centuries.

So now here we are, living into our eighties, nineties, and even beyond. And suddenly we're struck with all these diseases for which there is no known cure.

For instance, after heart disease and cancer, the biggest killer right now is Alzheimer's disease. This primarily affects people in their eighties, though it can hit at any age. About 2 to 3 percent of people aged sixty-five exhibit some sign of the disease, but about 25 to 50 percent of people aged eighty-five experience some form of it. I say "some form" because not only is there no known cure, there's no really easy way to diagnose it. It's a silent killer in that it sneaks up on you slowly, starting with short-term memory loss and increasing apathy to the environment around you. An inability to learn new information is also an early sign of the disease. Later forms include much more severe, longer-term memory loss, an inability to recall basic facts, reduced language skills and fluency, and a degradation of basic motor skills. Ultimately this leads to complete loss of memory, motor skills, and eventually the ability to eat and breathe, causing death. For Alzheimer's victims, inception to death takes, on average, seven years, with very few lasting more than fourteen years.

The care and treatment of Alzheimer's patients costs the United States more than $100 billion annually, with 5.7 million Americans currently diagnosed with the disease. This number has been increasing at a rate of about 3.4 percent annually, but that rate will itself increase with the aging Baby Boomer population, combined with an ever-increasing average life span. In fact, the Alzheimer's Association estimates that up to 14 million of the 76 million Baby Boomers will experience some form of the disease.

Given such a strong trend, it only stands to reason that we should look for a way to benefit from it, following the standard forever portfolio procedure:

- **Identify the trend.** The increased number of people who will get Alzheimer's, and the need for additional money and resources to care for these patients, should be a strong enough trend over the next fifty years to make this an investable opportunity.
- **Identify the companies that play this trend**—those working on Alzheimer's treatments and services.
- **Invest in a basket of these companies,** focusing more allocation on companies with strong balance sheets, other sources of revenue, and stronger investors already behind them. With a diverse yet strong group like this, if any of them develop a cure, then the returns will be multiples of the investment. If none of them do, then the other sources of revenue, the strong balance sheets, and the interest of superinvestors should still bear out the soundness of this investment.

The one speculative play here is Myriad Genetics (MYGN), because the company at this point does not make money and probably will not until it completes the FDA trials of its Alzheimer's treatment. Myriad is (as of this writing) in phase III clinical trials for the Alzheimer's drug Flurizan, after phase II demonstrated that the drug was relatively safe. Flurizan works by reducing levels of a toxic peptide, amyloid beta 42, which kills neurons and creates the plaque found in the brains of Alzheimer's patients. In nonclinical studies, the drug appears to reduce the levels of this peptide.

The company, with a current market cap of $1.7 billion, does have some revenues while working on this treatment. It sells diagnostic tools to help detect breast, ovarian, and other cancers. With currently

$180 million cash in the bank and a burn of only $17 million, Myriad appears to have enough cash to survive the finish of the phase III trials. If the trial pays off, it could start to make a dent in the $100 billion Alzheimer's market.

Wyeth (WYE) is a much larger pharmaceutical company that's also working on a drug for Alzheimer's: AAB-001, codeveloped with Elan (ELN). It is in phase II trials. Wyeth has $22 billion in revenues and sells medicines for every disease known to mankind. The company now also trades for only 11 times earnings. As Warren Buffett often says, "If a company is going to be here twenty years from now, then it's probably a good buy right now." With $6 billion in cash flow, $13 billion of cash in the bank, and 10 percent average annual growth over the past five years, this company is probably here to stay. And if it can succeed in the FDA trials for AAB-001, then the market potential will ensure that an investment with Wyeth succeeds.

Eli Lilly (LLY) is also developing an Alzheimer's drug, LY450139, which is in phase II trials. This is another mega pharmaceutical company that will benefit from many of the trends discussed in this book that will affect aging Baby Boomers over the next decades. Eli Lilly develops drugs to cure or treat illnesses ranging from erectile dysfunction and bipolar disorder to cancer.

Before a cure for Alzheimer's disease is found, it's important to recognize that there are some natural ways to slow the progression of Alzheimer's. After all, you want to be around as long as possible to enjoy the rewards of your forever portfolio.

In a 2007 paper in *Neurology*, "Mediterranean Diet and Alzheimer Disease Mortality," the authors suggest that a diet of fruit and vegetables, bread, wheat and other cereals, olive oil, fish, and red wine may reduce the risk of Alzheimer's or at least delay its onset. And in a 2003 article in the *New England Journal of Medicine*, "Leisure Activities and the Risk of Dementia in the Elderly," the authors suggest that intellectual activities such as crossword puzzles or chess could postpone the onset of Alzheimer's.

With that in mind, try the crossword puzzle I created for this book.

I don't know if it will slow any developing cases of Alzheimer's, but it should be fun and increase your knowledge of the investing world.

THE FOREVER PORTFOLIO PUZZLE
JAMES ALTUCHER

Across

4 Dairy Queen owner
6 Where to find the cheapest mortgage rate
7 Created the pushup bra and a multibillion-dollar defense company
12 Steve Jobs is the largest shareholder
13 Oldest company in the Dow under the same name
14 Mathematician turned mega hedge fund manager in Manhattan
17 The richest college dropout

Down

1 Largest publicly traded mutual fund company
2 Buffett's number two owns this newspaper chain
3 Author of *The Madness of Crowds*
5 The longest-running columnist for *Forbes* and mega money manager
8 Buffett piled in after bogus salad oil ruined everything

Across (continued)

18 This company started the South Sea Bubble
19 Always known for breaking pounds
22 Tech company started by Buffett's office building neighbor
23 Company with largest number of patents in auto safety sector
26 How to create your own online poker casino
30 Oldest U.S. bank
33 A trillion-dollar market-cap company in 2007, briefly
36 Buffett delivered their newspapers
38 Charges 50 percent management fee, his hedge fund is named after his initials (last name)
39 Sunglasses from Brooks Brothers are under this shade
40 Cramer's partner at his hedge fund
41 CEO of acquired company in biggest bad deal
42 When you don't want to read books anymore (company)
44 Crackers, and also runs the *Washington Post*
45 Where internet.com lives
46 The online exchange for wrecked cars
47 Acquirer in biggest bad deal of the past century
49 1920s economist and superinvestor
50 First dot-com company
52 Briefly became the richest man in the world in 2007
53 Inflation at male-only party
54 Hedge fund manager who bet against subprime in 2007 and made billions
55 This flower was also a bubble

Down (continued)

9 Munger's chairman of this insurance company
10 Former SPAC with delicious drink
11 Longest-running *Forbes* columnist's father, a famous investor
15 Company with most consecutive years of raising dividend
16 Warren Buffett's number two
18 Largest chocolate company in the world
20 Bought the company that bought the Waldorf-Astoria
21 Rogue trader of 2007
24 Super mathematician turned mega hedge fund manager on Long Island
25 Bought stock in the crash of 1907
27 Company featured in *Liar's Poker*
28 The other author of *Security Analysis*
29 CEO of bad acquirer in biggest bad deal
31 Former Morgan Stanley top exec who went *Hedgehogging*
32 Sometime world's richest man is a large shareholder of wireless company American _____
34 Originally called the Bank of Italy
35 Decided that even banks deserve a holiday
37 The root of all Internet registrars
42 Mega hedge fund DE Shaw owner left to start this
43 Carnegie Mellon–spawned search engine from the '90s
48 His girlfriend helped him make billions with her Pez dispensers
49 Before Sears, Eddie Lampert shopped here
51 Yet Another Hierarchical Officious Oracle

See page 245 for answers

GOUT

While we're on the subject of diseases with no known cure, we should also discuss gout, which is a form of rheumatoid arthritis. Gout occurs when the body has levels of uric acid higher than the kidneys can process. The uric acid then builds up deposits in the joints, causing gout—and considerable pain.

Gout is related to obesity. Studies have shown that obesity tends to cause sleep apnea, and the resultant oxygen deprivation tends to prevent the breakdown of uric acid. Usually, gout symptoms appear before severe sleep apnea symptoms, but it's the apnea that causes the gout. Hence, it's likely that the incidence of gout will rise along with that of obesity over the next fifty years. Since there's no known cure, it's worth noting that a good diet can prevent gout, particularly among those who might have a predisposition toward it due to a high body-mass index. Specifically, reducing intake of alcohol (particularly beer) and sugary soft drinks, drinking more water, and keeping meat, seafood, and tofu to moderate levels, all could prevent the onset of gout.

How can we invest in this trend? GlaxoSmithKline (GSK) makes Zylprim (allopurinol), which helps alleviate the symptoms of gout attacks. GSK's gout medicines are not going to be a big factor in its $45 billion in revenues, but this is another company that trades at an abnormally low multiple over its earnings and yet will have nonstop demand for its products from the aging Baby Boomer population.

ASTHMA

Nobody really understands why, but the number of children developing asthma increases every year. The number of cases in the United States has gone from 5 million in 1980 to almost 20 million in 2008. The statistics are frightening: The American Lung Association estimates that 24.5 million workdays are missed due to adult asthma attacks, and $1.7 billion in lost productivity per year is due to asthma-related deaths. Children with asthma missed 9 million schooldays in 2002 and made 2 million emergency room visits in 2001.

Why is the problem getting worse? The authors of a 2008 paper, "Ozone, Oxidant Defense Genes, and Risk of Asthma During Adolescence," suggest that air pollution, holes in the ozone layer, and generally poor air quality has increased the prevalence of asthma among children. And the authors of "Does Antibiotic Exposure During Infancy Lead to Development of Asthma? A Systematic Review and Metaanalysis" suggest that increased antibiotic use may weaken children's immune systems in such a way as to bring about the onset of asthma. These theories in turn predict that the rural-to-urban trend occurring in developing countries will also lead to increased asthma there over the next twenty years.

As always, when picking companies that are working on treatments for asthma, I check out what the superinvestors are loading up on. In his Q1 2008 filing, George Soros's biggest new investment was in a company I never heard of, MAP Pharmaceuticals (MAPP), which is developing a new nebulizer that relies less on corticosteroids to reduce the effects of asthma attacks. The drug is currently in phase III trials with the FDA. The company has several asthma products in the pipeline, all in various stages of FDA trials. The fact that MAP has, as of mid-2008, $90 million in cash and only a $30 million burn gives me some confidence (particularly with an investor like Soros doing research) that it can survive the trials and produce good results.

In the less speculative realm, several large pharmaceutical companies, including Schering-Plough (SGP) and GlaxoSmithKline, make asthma inhalers currently in use and also have strong franchises in other sectors of health care. Any investments in the "no cure" index of your forever portfolio should include some of these big pharmas as well as some speculative plays.

10

Drink Clean Water

Global warming is an interesting topic that I'm more or less avoiding, despite this being a book about global demographic trends occurring over the next fifty years. In a sense, I'm avoiding the topic because of the controversy. Why avoid something because of controversy? Isn't it by wading through the murky depths of debate that one can find opportunity? In most situations, yes, but probably not in this one. When it comes to global warming, there's simply too much debate, too much politics, too much career ambition at stake for the people involved. Since this is a book not necessarily about controversy but, at its root, on how to sleep soundly with your investment portfolio, tackling the global warming controversy is beyond its scope.

But just for the heck of it, here are some of the questions being debated:

Is global warming caused by humans, or is it part of a natural cycle of the Earth?

What are the effects of global warming?

What can we do about any of these effects?

Is global warming reversible?

There is no definitive scientific consensus as to the answers to any of the questions above. And the debates have been brutal, even potentially career ending, depending what side you're on. Even just including these paragraphs in this book will guarantee endless hate mail from people on either side of the equation, all of whom will insist that scientific consensus on the above issues is not in dispute at all.

This is not to say I'm a skeptic on global warming—I'm not saying anything one way or the other. But part of the approach of this book is to focus on understanding ideas that are clearly beyond dispute, concepts in which the math and science are fairly easy to grasp, areas where superinvestors (or, let's say, experts who are far smarter than I am on a topic) clear the path for me to place strong bets and rest easy at night. Global warming is just not there yet in terms of its consensus or how the investors should best treat it. And, as with defense companies, it's often the politics of the day that determine which global warming–related companies or issues will rule the day (but that day only). So I'll pass on making investment recommendations for now.

Still, it's useful to at least air the debates briefly before attending to the actual topic at hand—clean water—because it is related to global warming, at least superficially.

First of all, who believes global warming is not related to human activity? Many, if not most, scientists do posit that global warming is related to the burning of fossil fuels and deforestation, two human activities dear to my New Jersey–native heart. Naomi Oreskes, a professor at the University of California–San Diego, in a 2004 essay in *Science* magazine, surveyed 928 academic papers that all agree global warming is caused by the above activities. However, various other articles, including a 2006 op-ed piece in the *Wall Street Journal* by Richard Lindzen, a professor of meteorology at MIT, have questioned this study and maintained that many opponents to the popular views on global warming have not published their work for fear of future funding difficulty or ostracism by the scientific community. While this view seems rather paranoid, I still don't want to dip my finger into the middle of a boiling cauldron. There are enough alternative hypotheses to suggest that the human cause is suspect:

- Urban areas have become more crowded. More people equals more body heat. Measurement stations in urban areas could show significant warming.
- There's some evidence that warming is related to variations in solar activity. John Carlisle, in his paper "Sun to Blame for Global Warming" (the National Center for Public Policy Research, June 1998), claims that temperatures have also been rising on Mars, Venus, other planets, and the moon. Most likely, humans are not the cause of those temperature rises.

Again, I'm just presenting a couple of alternatives here, not arguing for them. For each theory, there are dozens of papers and opinions explaining or rejecting it. There are also several alternative explanations for human causation of global warming.

However, let's say there is global warming and it's caused by humans. Well, what do we do about it? Do we need to care?

In 2001, the American Association of State Climatologists stated that even if there is climate change, it's incredibly difficult to predict the impact of that change. Here is part of its statement:

> Climate prediction is difficult because it involves complex, nonlinear interactions among all components of the earth's environmental system. . . . The AASC recognizes that human activities have an influence on the climate system. Such activities, however, are not limited to greenhouse-gas forcing and include changing land use and sulfate emissions, which further complicate the issue of climate prediction.

Furthermore, climate predictions have not demonstrated skill in projecting future variability and changes in such important climate conditions as growing season, drought, flood-producing rainfall, heat waves, tropical cyclones and winter storms. These are the type of events that have a more significant impact on society than annual average global temperature trends. Policy responses to climate variability and change should be flexible and sensible. The difficulty of prediction and the impossibility of verification of predictions decades into the future are important factors that allow for competing views of the long-term climate future. Therefore, the AASC recommends that policies related to long-term climate not be based on particular predictions, but instead should focus on policy alternatives that make sense for a wide range of plausible climatic conditions regardless of future climate.

However, one phenomenon we're fairly certain of is that, whatever the reasons are, some global warming is occurring. That warming may not amount to much, but it accounts for almost 1 degree Celsius warmer global average temperatures over the past five decades.

All of this is an extensive, but necessary, introduction to the issue of clean water and its scarcity on Earth. Regardless of causes and even regardless of impact, the slight rise in global temperature only fuels a fire that is already raging: the dwindling of the so-called "blue gold" of the twenty-first century—water.

Let's get a little scared first, since that will force us to consider the significant impact of this issue. Clearly, there is no shortage of water in the world—70 percent of the planet's surface is covered by it. However, 97 percent of that water is either polluted or contains salt, which renders it largely unusable without processing. And of the remaining 3 percent, very little is easily accessible, as most of it is trapped within the polar ice caps. The World Health Organization has estimated that perhaps only 1 percent of that 3 percent is available for use as potable water. Meanwhile, several related issues are facing us:

- A growing global economy has created opportunities in urban areas for people from rural areas, causing greater water consumption in cities than they were originally built to handle. The country with the greatest rural-to-urban emigration, China, has the same amount of water as Canada but more than one hundred times the population, which is why over half of China's inhabitants consume water containing greater-than-permissible levels of animal and human waste. This may also be one reason why China faces the highest liver- and stomach-cancer death rates in the world.

- Since 1950, the world's population has doubled, but worldwide consumption of water has tripled.

- In developing nations, 80 percent of all diseases can be attributed to consumption of unclean water. And throughout the world, 50 percent of all hospital beds are filled by people sick from water-related illnesses.

- No technological development can replace water. Gas-fueled cars, for instance, can ultimately be replaced by battery- or ethanol-powered cars. According to Summit Global Management, "One can substitute wheat for oats, coal for natural gas, corn oil for soybean oil and hydroelectricity for fossil-fuel generated power, but . . . water has no substitute regardless of price, the only element in the world of which this is true: This most fundamental of facts is another key to the inexorable and intractable demand for water that will not abate with time."

- According to Eric Fry at the *Daily Reckoning*, "The UN estimates that in less than 25 years, if present water consumption trends continue, five billion people will be living in areas where it will be impossible—or nearly impossible—to meet basic water needs for sanitation, cooking and drinking. But present

trends simply cannot continue. The human toll is already hor-
rifying, and the economic toll is rising rapidly."

It's not surprising that there are several features of an investment
in the water space that are attractive. Inflation, recession, depression,
or war will not affect the demand for water. Water companies have a
history of good market performance regardless of market conditions.
And there are several types of companies that are engaged in the
ongoing battle to fight the unclean-water trend:

Water utilities. These are the companies that take the water and distribute it through pipes, ultimately to your faucet. I'll get into specific companies below, but suffice it to say that a good investment
approach here is to find a smattering of water utilities with various
characteristics:

- A decent dividend: Just like electric utilities, water utilities have
  very predictable cash flows and can often afford greater-than-
  normal dividends as a result.
- A good investor base (the typical forever-portfolio approach).
- Diversification: Seek water utilities not just in the United States
  but also ones that cover various emerging economies.

Treatment companies. These are companies that take water from a
nonpotable source, apply treatment to the water, and convert it into
a usable form. This can range from companies that do desalination
to companies that treat polluted water.

Monitoring companies. Firms in this realm sell equipment to detect
for chemicals and pollutants in a water supply. Since 9/11, this has
been an important issue, due to concerns about terrorists contami-
nating large water sources, such as rivers or reservoirs.

Infrastructure companies. These businesses make the pipes, pumps, valves, storage tanks, and other equipment that are used to set up a water system. Right now, the United States has an estimated 800,000 pipelines delivering water, and the average age of these pipes is forty-three years. It's estimated that the life expectancy for most pipes is about fifty years, suggesting that a massive overhaul looms, which will make use of these infrastructure companies.

Water resource management. Let's say a country needs to completely update an antiquated water infrastructure. It can hire a consulting company specializing in water resource management to manage the project for them.

Conglomerates. Keep an eye out for companies like GE, which is entering all the arenas described above.

I've basically plagiarized the above categories of water companies from the prospectus of the PowerShares Water Resources (PHO). This is a publicly traded ETF based on the Palisades Water Index, which attempts to track the companies comprising the burgeoning water industry.

Perhaps the company with the greatest revenues in the clean-water space is General Electric (GE), which has been rolling up companies in every category. However, the effect this has on the overall performance of GE stock is minimal at this point, because clean-water income accounts for less than 10 percent of overall company revenues.

Here are some other clean-water companies that are worth a look: Calgon Carbon Corporation (CCC) is in the water-filtration business, part of the treatment category.

CALGON CARBON CORP.

as of Apr. 23, 2008

Splits: ▼

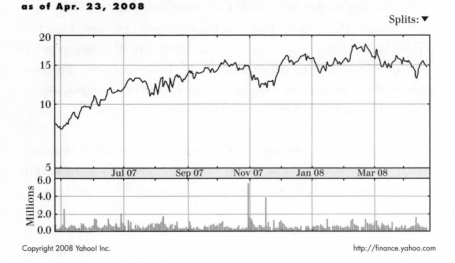

Consolidated Water Company (CWCO) provides services in all of the categories of the clean-water space, specifically in the Cayman Islands, Belize, Barbados, the British Virgin Islands, and the Bahamas.

CONSOLIDATED WATER CO., INC.

as of Apr. 24, 2008

Splits: ▼

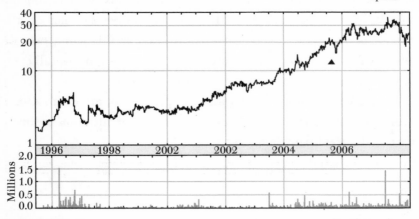

Pentair (PNR) is in the infrastructure and treatment segment, and it provides filtration systems, pumps, pipes, valves, and storage tanks.

PENTAIR, INC.
as of Apr. 24, 2008

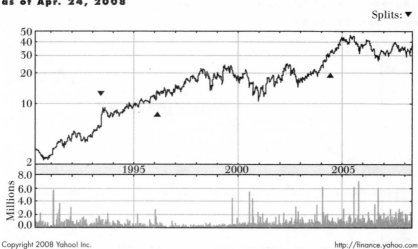

Copyright 2008 Yahoo! Inc.   http://finance.yahoo.com

Companhia de Saneamento Basico do Estado de São Paulo (SBS) supplies and treats water for the São Paulo region of Brazil.

COMPANHIA DE SANEAMENTO BASICO DO ESTADO DE SÃO PAULO,
as of Apr. 24, 2008

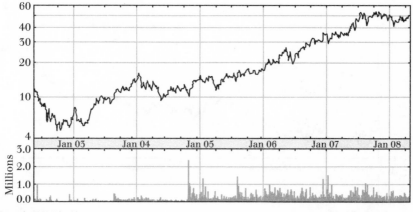

Copyright 2008 Yahoo! Inc.   http://finance.yahoo.com

The California Water Services Group (CWT) services the western United States, and one nice feature (as of this writing) is that it carries a 3.3 percent dividend.

CALIFORNIA WATER SERVICES GROUP
as of Apr. 21, 2008

Splits: ▼

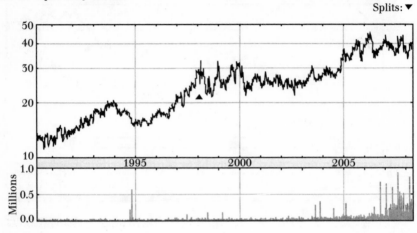

http://finance.yahoo.com

Valmont Industries (VMI), a Nebraska-based company, makes irrigation systems.

VALMONT INDUSTRIES, INC.
as of Apr. 24, 2008

Splits: ▼

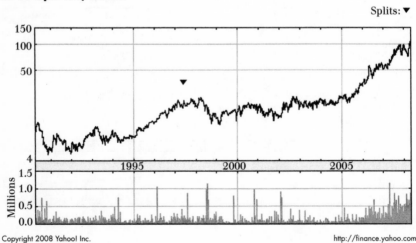

http://finance.yahoo.com

The American States Water Company (AWR) is a California-based utility involved in the purchase, production, and distribution of water.

AMERICAN STATES WATER COMPANY
as of Apr. 24, 2008

Splits: ▼

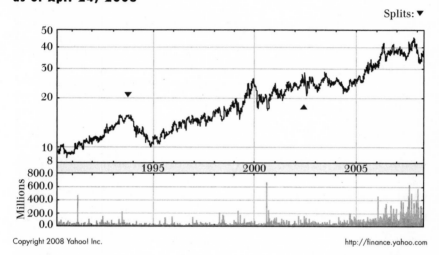

Copyright 2008 Yahoo! Inc.   http://finance.yahoo.com

Idexx Laboratories (IDXX) makes products to test water for biological contaminants. As of this writing, the stock is owned by several of the hedge funds and mutual funds that I like to piggyback, including Jim Simons's Renaissance Technologies, the Sequoia Fund, and the Royce Funds. My suspicion is that this company is their hedge against terrorism. Note for all of these companies that they've performed well in both bull and bear markets.

Renaissance is also a shareholder in Veolia Environment ADS (VE), which provides water-resource management services.

IDEXX LABORATORIES, INC.

as of Apr. 24, 2008

Splits: ▼

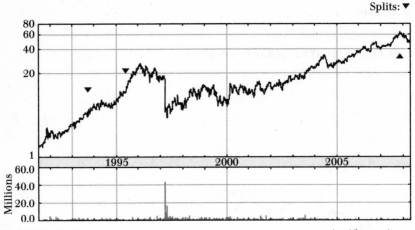

Copyright 2008 Yahoo! Inc.   http://finance.yahoo.com

VEOLIA ENVIRONMENT, ADS

as of Apr. 24, 2008

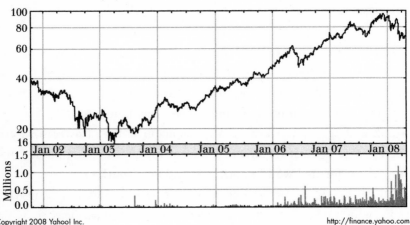

Copyright 2008 Yahoo! Inc.   http://finance.yahoo.com

Jacobs Engineering Group (JEC) makes most of its fortune by offering services to the oil and gas industries. But it's now applying the
same engineering skills involved in setting up oil-drilling infrastructure to establishing irrigation systems and infrastructure. One person who keeps JEC on my radar is superinvestor T. Boone Pickens.

Pickens made an enormous amount of money from 2004 to 2007 by making a big bet on peak oil theory, which predicts the fluctuations in supply and price as the world runs out of oil. It's that bet that kept him fully diversified across the range of oil and oil-services companies while the price leapt from $30 to $100 a barrel. Now he's getting into water, having set up Mesa Water to buy water rights throughout Texas. Pickens has stated that he hopes to make more than $1 billion on his $75 million investment in Mesa. Meanwhile, through his hedge fund, BP Capital, he has become an investor in JEC.

JACOBS ENGINEERING GROUP, INC.
as of Apr. 24, 2008

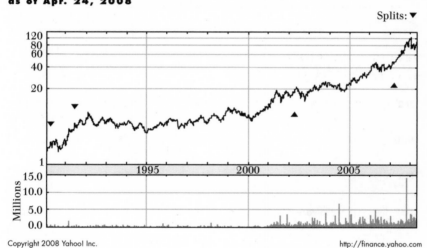

http://finance.yahoo.com

Most of Pickens's current holdings (as of mid-2008) are oil-related, but I predict that bit by bit he'll get into water. Here is the complete list of his current holdings according to j3sg.com:

BP CAPITAL HOLDINGS

Ticker	Company	New/ Closed	Last Close	Value (thousands)	Shares Held
SU	Suncor Energy (USA)	-	$97.73	$170,423	1,797,523
XOM	ExxonMobil	New	$85.49	$151,824	1,640,276
RIG	Transocean	-	$131.29	$102,608	907,631
OXY	Occidental Petroleum	-	$70.13	$96,320	1,503,115
CVX	Chevron	New	$82.12	$89,689	958,424
SLB	Schlumberger	-	$84.89	$81,965	780,615
DNR	Denbury Resources, Inc.	-	$28.59	$146,434	3,276,662
ABB	ABB Ltd. (ADR)	-	$24.11	$68,502	2,611,596
JEC	Jacobs Engineering Group	-	$78.53	$66,184	875,687
SGR	Shaw Group	-	$60.52	$54,471	937,532
FLR	Fluor	-	$122.27	$53,578	372,122
GSF	GlobalSantaFe	-	$86.83	$52,235	687,122
TLM	Talisman Energy (USA)	-	$15.95	$40,075	2,034,259 .
FWLT	Foster Wheeler	New	$71.82	$79,126	602,720
TIE	Titanium Metals	-	$22.69	$35,672	1,062,926
DRC	Dresser-Rand Group	-	$35.05	$34,699	812,434
IOC	InterOil (USA)	-	$20.60	$29,829	943,964

% of Portfolio	Value Change (thousands)	Change In Shares Held	% of Company	Industry
13.07%	11,378	28,784	0.392755	Oil & gas refining
11.64%	151,824	1,640,276	0.0288101	Integrated oil & gas
7.87%	8,111	15,986	0.310981	Oil & gas drilling
7.38%	40,592	540,298	0.179348	Independent oil & gas
6.88%	89,689	958,424	0.0445937	Integrated oil & gas
6.28%	16,721	12,500	0.0654844	Oil & gas equipment
11.23%	12,763	52,472	1.34141	Independent oil & gas
5.25%	10,425	41,822	0.129287	Industrial electrical
5.07%	16,630	14,024	0.740226	Heavy construction
4.18%	17,393	136,543	1.15572	Industrial equipment
4.11%	24,709	112,905	0.420833	Heavy construction
4.00%	3,385	11,003	0.303657	Oil & gas drilling
3.07%	3,262	129,800	0.188357	Independent oil & gas
6.07%	39,563	602,720	0.419511	Residential construction
2.73%	17,846	504,115	0.655354	Industrial metals
2.66%	−10,555	−333,245	0.946672	Diversified machinery
2.29%	22,512	557,665	3.24833	Oil & gas refining

Ticker	Company	New/ Closed	Last Close	Value (thousands)	Shares Held
KBR	KBR	-	$31.91	$23,362	602,582
GBX	Greenbrier	-	$27.77	$14,941	559,382
WFT	Weatherford International	-	$66.35	$12,691	188,911
APC	Anadarko Petroleum	-	$59.49	$12,544	233,371
VLO	Valero Energy	Closed	$59.20	$0	0
TSO	Tesoro Petroleum	Closed	$37.38	$0	0

% of Portfolio	Value Change (thousands)	Change In Shares Held	% of Company	Industry
1.79%	14,694	272,135	0.356581	N/A
1.15%	−1,693	8,940	3.45831	Railroads
0.97%	2,423	3,025	0.0558644	Oil & gas equipment
0.96%	615	3,921	0.0500412	Independent oil & gas
0%	−30,722	−415,954	0	Oil & gas refining
0%	−13,875	−242,781	0	Oil & gas refining

11

The Boring Forever Portfolio

O ne of the keys to having a forever portfolio is to live as long as you possibly can. One of the keys to living a long and productive life is to enjoy what you do. There's no two ways about it. One way you can enjoy what you do is if you are either helping people, another is attempting to do something that's never been done before. So put aside stocks for a second, although I'll circle back to that momentarily. I live and breathe stocks. I've run funds, funds of funds, and I've been a trader for hedge funds as well as a day trader for myself. But it hasn't always been about stocks for me.

Eleven years ago, I approached HBO with an idea: Your network, I said, was the first and the best in the cable TV world at launching original programming. How about doing the same for the Internet, with an original Web show?

This was the pre-YouTube, pre-blog era. The idea I pitched HBO was called III:am. Get it? Three a.m. The basic concept was that if you were out and about at three in the morning on a Tuesday night (or technically, Wednesday morning), then there was something going on. Why aren't you sleeping? Don't you have to work the next day, or go to school? To HBO's credit, they let me do it. Can you imagine? Getting paid to go out at three in the morning and having carte blanche to go up to everybody I saw and say, "Hey, I'm with HBO, can I ask you what you're doing right now?"

So every week, I went out with a camera crew. I'd stop everyone I could find in the East Village, the Meatpacking District, everyplace in New York City from Wall Street to Rikers Island (the largest jail). For two years, I basically turned over every rock on the pavement, interviewing drug dealers, prostitutes, their customers, and everyone in between, then put up the videos, along with transcriptions, photos, and a unique design, on HBO.com. Not only was III:am a hugely popular site during its two-year run, but it was also unbelievably fun, and it changed my life. I saw the craziest things I'll ever see, and I did the show for 104 straight episodes until my increasing need for sleep won out.

Each week, I would post four pictures to the III:am site from what I considered the best recent interviews. Very early on, I realized the key to page views on the Internet: People only clicked on pictures of blonde women—or blonde transvestites (in fact, sometimes even more on the transvestites). Prostitutes who were also blonde? Those would be the biggest page views of the month. When I put my own picture up there? Single-digit page views.

When people go online, they want flash, they want scandal, they want excitement. For seven days in a row now, either Paris Hilton or Lindsay Lohan has been on the front page of the *New York Post*. Scoff all you want, but the *Post* is one of the only newspapers in the top one hundred that's increasing circulation year over year.

The same thing goes for stocks. Everyone wants to talk about Google or Dendreon. I know this because I see what people click on at Stockpickr.com, a MySpace for finance that I set up that's now owned by TheStreet.com. For a while it was Sirius and XMSR; those were the big page-view winners. But now Dendreon is gold, with Google a close runner-up and, believe it or not, NYX.

But let's look beyond the glitz to find some value. As a rule, always consider the most boring stocks imaginable. These are companies so dull they can't even get three or four characters in their ticker symbols. Heck, they can't even get two characters—stocks like A (Agilent Technologies) or B (Barnes Group). M was recently given to Macy's; Microsoft didn't want it—too boring, Steve Ballmer supposedly said to a shoeshine boy. If you want stocks that last for the long run, you have to consistently avoid glitzy stocks with "personality," the ones that the pundits talk about every day on TV or in the newspaper. The dull stocks I am talking about work now, and they will work for the next fifty years. How can you find them? Start with the single letters. They've got staying power.

I like Barnes Group for instance, even though you can't find a more boring company. I can't describe what it does here or you'll put down the book. Suffice it to say that Barnes supplies very specific parts for airplane engines and replacement parts for railroads. The company started in 1857, during the dot-com boom of the 1850s— railroads. It was literally the picks and shovels of the railroad boom. Now, B is a great backdoor way to play the current railroad boom, which guys like Buffett have been predicting with his purchase of rail-line companies such as Union Pacific and Burlington Northern. Barnes trades right now at a forward P/E of just 13, and obviously has done a good job of surviving no matter what the market conditions.

I also like Agilent Technologies. HPQ analysts were falling asleep during conference calls until Hewlett-Packard decided to spin off Agilent into its own company. It makes measurement tools—don't worry about the specifics. This was the original Hewlett-Packard started in the fabled Silicon Valley garage, not in 1998 but in 1938. The company trades at 7.5 times cash flows, and I believe it will end its story as a public company by doing an LBO in the near future.

Rather than go through all the other single-letter stocks, let's just look at the ones that haven't been taken yet (just in case you want one): G (which was Gillette until recently), I, J, L, N, P, U, V, W, and Z.

Meanwhile, as your portfolio gets solid and dull, a great vacation idea: if you live in a city, don't waste your money traveling to a different city. Just sleep from 9 a.m. to 8 p.m. every day for a week and hang out outside from 10 p.m. to 5 a.m. It will be a complete reversal of what you are used to, with all the normal routines of daily life shed for that week. You might even meet some fun people.

12

The Baby Boomers

I f there's only one trend you pay attention to during the next fifty years, this should be it: 76 million Baby Boomers are retiring over the next decade, and they need a lot of help. They need to continue to look young, and they need to enjoy life as much as possible. More and more of them will gamble, and they will all need some form of health care. Not only that, most of them have a secret desire to live forever.

WHO ARE THE BABY BOOMERS?

After World War II, the United States experienced an explosion in births as American soldiers returned home. Sociologists define this group of children born between 1946 and 1964 as the Baby Boom generation. Not all people born on the fringes of this time period consider themselves Boomers, however, and as a society we typically correlate the Baby Boom generation with the 1960s, the decade they came of age. I'm not sure what the current generation (kids coming of age right now) are being labeled, but I know I was in the so-called Generation X—originally known for its laziness, but now we all know we were just waiting for the Internet to wake us up.

In 1946, the estimated population of the United States was 141 million. Today we've more than doubled that at roughly 298 million. Boomers currently represent 28 percent of the population, with a total of 76.1 million people between the ages of thirty-two and fifty back in 1996. Between 1940 and 1994, 202 million Americans were born; during the sixteen years of the Baby Boom, approximately 75.8 million Americans were born. In other words, the birth rate was about 25 percent higher than in the generations before and after.

More than 4 million people turned fifty in 2006, and the oldest of the Baby Boomers turned sixty. Every hour now, 330 people cross the threshold to their sixties. In 2005, life expectancy hit an all-time-high of 75.4 years for men and 80.5 years for women. This is up considerably from 1900, when men could only expect to live 47.9 years and women 50.7.

Boomers are also significantly more educated than previous generations. In 1947, out of all adults aged twenty-five and older, only 33 percent had a high school diploma and only 5 percent had at least a bachelor's degree. This is a big discrepancy compared to 2004, with 85 percent having a high school diploma and 28 percent having at least a bachelor's degree.

Although births have been slowly increasing since 1977, this is not considered a boom. The reason for this is that many Boomers waited longer to have children than their parents did. The next "boom" has been more evenly spread out through the years, and some Boomers have decided not to have children. This indicates that the Baby Boomer phenomenon may have been a onetime event, and therefore you shouldn't wait to capitalize on it.

Let's examine the Baby Boomers in more detail. During 2005,

50.8 percent of them were women. The average woman can expect to live longer than ever before; older women will continue to outnumber men, and this gender gap will increase with age. In 2003, the female-to-male ratio was 11:5 for the 65–69 age group and 22:6 for the 85-and-over age group. This is not a pleasant statistic for me, being a man. I mean, I wouldn't want it to be reversed, but I wish it were more equal. I'm forty now, and I want to be able to enjoy a forever portfolio by getting to the ages mentioned above.

Now it's time to take a look at what the people who survive will spend. The size of the elderly population is projected to increase in all states over the next twenty years. In the next few sections we will look at some of the trends this will lead to, plus some of the opportunities for taking advantage of them.

13

The U.S. Gambling Industry

Why do people like to gamble? In almost all cases, the odds are stacked against you. That means you'll lose money in the long run, no matter what your system is, no matter what game you play. Everybody thinks they can count cards in blackjack. Get over it. You can't. And, in poker, everyone thinks they are better than their buddies at bluffing. Guess what? You aren't.

If you are playing a casual game of poker with your friends, there's one way to guarantee winning: Don't bluff.

Just say no to bluffing. It's a horrible addiction that will bleed money out of your wallet and your bank account. When you play a game with friends, at some point in the evening everyone starts playing mostly every hand. Fine. Let them do that. Then you play only your best hands. They'll all start bluffing because they think they can bluff you out. Sometimes they will, but most of the time they can't, because you're only playing good hands. Try not to draw for a better hand. Remember the saying, "Those who draw for straights and flushes arrive in cars and go home in buses." Once you have a decent hand, stay in until the end, bet every round, and don't spend all your winnings in one place.

I went through a phase in 1998 when I played poker every single day for a year. I'm not exaggerating. For 365 straight days, I played poker from 8 p.m. to 4 a.m. every night, mostly at the Mayfair Club, which was on Twenty-fifth Street in Manhattan until Mayor Giuliani had it shut down. This was prior to the poker craze that swept the world once the World Series of Poker and the World Poker Tour were televised. During the days, I'd read books, memorize or work out the statistics of the different types of hands, think about strategies, and watch videos of the different great players to see how they operated.

Why did I enjoy playing? It wasn't about the money at all. Most of the time I played against very good players, the type of people who played every single night for many more years than I had been playing or even been alive. I challenged myself by continually upping the stakes, and hence the quality of the player. Over time, I got better, but I never fooled myself into thinking I could make a living at it. I enjoyed the strategy of the game, the mental exhilaration, but more than anything, I loved the atmosphere. The game of poker comes with built-in friends: five to ten people sitting around a table all night, every single night, playing a game. Everyone is joking around and eating great food (the Mayfair had an excellent restaurant for club members). True, we were lying to each other all night long in attempts to take each other's hard-earned money. But that's often part of friendship in real life anyway, and this just put all the cards on the table, so to speak. I loved the visceral aspects of the game as well—holding the cards, flicking down a crappy hand, the feel of the chips.

Everybody has different reasons for gambling. True, it's an addiction, every bit as serious as any physical addiction. People want an outlet from the pain in their lives or the drudgery of working in a cubicle in an unsatisfying job. Gambling holds the genie that can release you from that, the big kill that puts you over the top so you can quit your job and change your life. And once you start losing money, there's always that feeling of "well, now I have to make it back." There have been plenty of books and discussions on what makes an addict and why one would get addicted to gambling as opposed to other activities. Suffice it to say, not only is gambling addictive, but as more and more cash is generated in a world of higher productivity and hence higher standards of living, more of that cash will be spent at casino tables, racetracks, lotteries, and Internet gambling sites.

Understanding the statistics of the different parts of the industry is crucial to building a portfolio, an investment strategy, and even entrepreneurial strategies that can take advantage of this trend over the next several decades.

Revenues from poker, for instance, increased in 2006, as Americans spent more than $238 million on organized poker in Nevada and New Jersey, a 15 percent increase over 2005 figures. There were 713 card rooms in five states, and from the four states that track card-room revenues, $1.1 billion was reported for 2006.

Fourteen percent of American adults played poker in 2006, whether in a casino or tournament (30 percent), while others played with friends and family. When survey respondents were asked if poker was a game of skill or chance, they were almost evenly split, with 45 percent considering it a game of skill and 41 percent calling it a game of chance. When asked why they play poker, more than half (58 percent) of respondents reported that the opportunity to spend time with friends and family is the primary reason they play. Less than one in ten (9 percent) cited the chance to win money.

Bugs Bunny would occasionally have an angel sitting on one shoulder and a devil on the other, and each one would be pulling on his ear, telling him what to do in critical situations. Virtue versus vice; vice versus virtue: They're the two opposing poles that attract us at every major decision point in our lives. Well, for the past five years, vice has been the winner. The Vice Fund, run by

Charles Norton, finished 2007 up over 17 percent in an otherwise difficult market. The five-year average annual return is 20 percent versus 13.5 percent for the Ave Maria Catholic Values Fund. Even keeping pace with the market is no small feat, but Vice has clearly pulled ahead, thanks to stalwart companies like Las Vegas Sands and cigarette maker R.J. Reynolds. I recently had a chance to sit down with Norton and dig a little further on how he, a self-described family man, finds value in vice.

Define vice.

The Vice Fund (VICEX) is really an alternative-sector strategy that focuses on the alcohol, tobacco, gaming, and defense industries, and we do so because we believe they offer true investment merit. By the way, many of the most widely held and well-known mutual-fund families own shares in companies engaged in the alcohol, tobacco, gaming, or defense businesses— Berkshire Hathaway is one of the largest holders of Anheuser-Busch. We just happen to focus exclusively on these four sectors.

Why is that an investment theme?

The ideology is simple: People around the globe have been drinking, smoking, and gambling for hundreds, if not thousands, of years. Wars have been around since the earliest hunter-gatherer societies. Few industry groups have a history that dates back that far. And no matter what is happening in the world economy, people will continue to drink, smoke, and gamble, and nations will need to defend themselves. As a result, in general, these companies tend to be steady performers in good times and bad—they are mostly insulated from economic slowdowns.

Besides the unvarying demand for their goods and services, there are other investment merits in the companies within these sectors. These businesses have high barriers to entry, and, in general, these companies are highly profitable with deep management teams. With regard to tobacco and alcohol specifically, the products are never made obsolete by a newer technology. And these businesses are global in nature; we have roughly 23 percent of our portfolio invested in foreign companies that trade in the U.S. via ADR, and many of the domestic firms we have a stake in operate internationally.

Do you think the Vice Fund presents a more attractive opportunity than funds like the Ave Maria "virtues" fund?

We do not perceive them as our competitors. It's a gray area. I should point out that many of the companies we own in the Vice Fund are stand-up corporate citizens.

What are some of your current holdings, and why are they cheap?

Our top holding right now is Altria Group (MO). The stock is trading at a significant, 20-plus-percent discount to the global consumer staples industry, despite in-line earnings growth prospects. I believe there are three issues that have depressed MO's valuation: litigation risk, its current corporate structure, and the uncertainty surrounding the timing of the breakup of the food and tobacco businesses. All of those issues are now largely removed, but the valuation still doesn't reflect that. On the litigation front, the industry has enjoyed a huge streak of defense verdicts. Today, the U.S. tobacco industry has a legal-risk profile comparable to other large-scale industries.

Las Vegas Sands (LVS) has been a core holding of ours for well over a year, and it's been a huge winner for our shareholders. The stock isn't cheap, but the growth potential here is off the charts. In 2004, Las Vegas Sands opened the first casino in Macao after the long-time monopoly was liberalized in 2001. Macao is just exploding—this year, only two short years after the first nonmonopoly casino opened, total Macao gaming revenue is going to surpass the Vegas Strip. The company recently expanded the Sands Macao and is developing the Cotai Strip. As a result, Las Vegas Sands will benefit tremendously as Macao goes from largely a VIP market to a mass market, and convention business booms. Elsewhere in Asia, Singapore ended a forty-year casino ban last year, and Las Vegas Sands will open the first casino there in 2009. And Japan and Thailand are also studying whether to allow casino gaming; Las Vegas Sands has already been in talks with Japanese officials. Today, roughly 60 percent of Las Vegas Sands's revenue and EBITDAR [earnings before taxes, depreciation, amortization, and rent] comes from Macao. All told, in the coming years, around 90 percent of revenue and EBITDAR will come from Asia.

On the alcoholic beverages side, our largest holding is Diageo (DEO), the leading premium spirits business in the world by volume, by net sales, and by operating profit; it also manages nine of the world's top twenty spirits brands. North America is experiencing the fastest growth in spirits volume in the world, as consumers are choosing spirits (and wine) over beer. The market leader in the fast-growing U.S. spirits market is Diageo, with about a quarter of the market. The company is a key supplier of liquor to Wal-Mart, which is aiming to aggressively boost its liquor sales, and it's buying back stock hand over fist.

What's your outlook for the U.S. economy over the next year, and how do you think the Vice Fund will behave in various economic climates?

The alcohol, tobacco, gaming, and defense sectors, in aggregate, are defensive in nature and tend to outperform the broad market in periods characterized by relatively low returns and periods with relative stagnancy, or worse, in the U.S. economy. Ironically, the Vice Fund was launched in August 2002 and has only operated in an economic expansion. It would logically seem that a defensive fund like the Vice Fund would lag the market in that environment, but in fact the Vice Fund has outperformed the S&P 500 and is in the top decile of all multicap core funds—over every time period, according to Lipper.

But the fact is, when the economy contracts, these sectors truly shine. And that is the precise environment we seem to be entering.

The economy is slowing rather dramatically, led by a sharp contraction in the housing market, and the yield curve's steep inversion suggests a recession cannot be entirely ruled out. The Fed chairman himself has said that the time lag from when a policy action is taken and when it's fully felt could be as long as eighteen months; there have been nine interest-rate hikes in the past eighteen months that might not have made their way through the system, so further slowing is a real possibility. And, of course, geopolitical tensions are high: conflicts in the Middle East, North Korea's missile tests, and Iran's nuclear arms intentions.

We think that with time and the changing economic environment, the Vice Fund will perform strongly in all seasons.

Do you use all the products you invest in?

> I'm a family man. My wife and I live in the Dallas suburbs with our three-year-old and infant daughters. I don't smoke, rarely gamble, and drink only on occasion. We are not making a political statement or advocating these activities in any way. Our job is to analyze the fundamentals of these businesses. We are very serious investors, and we take a very methodical, analytical approach in investing in these sectors.

If you're not familiar with the gambling industry, the stats are pretty impressive. Commercial casinos employed 366,000 people at the end of 2006, an increase of 3 percent over 2005. Gross gaming revenues at casinos exceeded $32 billion in 2006, which was a 6.8 percent increase over 2005. More than $5 billion of those revenues were paid back in the form of direct gaming taxes to the states and cities where commercial casinos are located; $13 billion of those revenues were paid to the 366,000 employees.

More than one-quarter (26 percent or 56.2 million people) of the U.S. adult population visited casinos in 2006, and they made more visits to casinos than in any previous year (371 million trips in 2006 compared to 322 million trips in 2005). The average number of trips per gambler also increased, from 6.1 in 2005 to 6.6 in 2006. Among American adults, a slightly higher percentage of males (32 percent) than females (29 percent) visited a casino in 2006.

The industry's growth can be attributed to continued expansion in existing commercial gaming states, the ongoing revitalization of the industry on the U.S. Gulf Coast after Hurricanes Katrina and Rita, and renovations and enhancements at existing properties in several key commercial gaming markets. During 2006, consumer spending in commercial casinos increased in every state. The largest gross gaming revenue increases occurred in Louisiana (+15.1 percent) and Nevada (+8.4 percent).

Increases in Louisiana were due to the local gaming industry's initial recovery from the impact of the hurricanes that interrupted business during 2005. Many believe that the casino industry will not only grow more quickly than the rest of the local economy in coming years, but also promote regional tourism. Increases in Nevada were due to continued growth and expansion in markets throughout the state.

More than one-quarter of the U.S. adult population visited a casino in 2006, according to Harrah's Entertainment/TNS polling data. Casino gambling maintains its position as the second-most-popular form of gambling, trailing only the lottery.

TOTAL COMMERCIAL CASINO REVENUES

Industry	2005 Gross Revenues (billions)
Card rooms	$1.12
Commercial casinos	$31.85
Charitable games and bingo	$2.33
Indian casinos	$22.62
Legal bookmaking	$0.1305
Lotteries	$22.89
Pari-mutuel wagering	$3.68
Total	$84.65

Source: Christiansen Capital Advisors LLC

CASINO REVENUES BY LOCATION

Location	2006 Revenues (millions)
Las Vegas Strip	$6,689.0
Atlantic City, NJ	$5,508.0
Chicagoland, IL	$2,595.0
Connecticut	$1,734.0

Location	2006 Revenues (millions)
Detroit, MI	$1,303.0
Tunica/Lula, MS	$1,252.0
St. Louis, MO/IL	$990.98
Reno/Sparks, NV	$939.50
Boulder Strip, NV	$929.70
Shreveport, LA	$847.18
Biloxi, MS	$845.2
Lawrenceburg/Rising Sun/ Elizabeth/Vevay, IN	$795.13
Kansas City, MO	$751.33
Lake Charles, LA	$656.85
Downtown Las Vegas	$630.29
Laughlin, NV	$629.76
Black Hawk, CO	$554.48
Council Bluffs, IA	$477.96
Charles Town, WV	$448.23

Source: Christiansen Capital Advisors LLC

Six U.S. casino markets (including a Native American casino market) had total gross gaming revenues of more than $1 billion in 2006. That year also saw a marked increase in gross gaming revenues in every market affected by the 2005 hurricanes, with Shreveport, New Orleans, and Lake Charles experiencing annual revenues higher than prestorm levels.

SPORTS BETTING AND ENTERTAINMENT

Sports betting also continued to grow in 2006. Bettors wagered more than $2.4 billion in Nevada sports books in 2006, with revenues from the activity totaling about 8 percent of the amount wagered.

A significant number of Americans also report taking advantage of an increasingly diverse array of nongaming amenities at casinos, including restaurants, live entertainment, and shopping. In fact, almost half (49 percent) of those surveyed said the food, shows, and everything else is more fun for them than the actual gambling. In 2005, 40 million people visited Las Vegas; half of them saw a big production show, spending more than $100 a person on tickets, totaling $2 billion for the casinos that house the theaters.

Survey results also indicate that overall acceptability of casino gambling remained high in 2006, with 82 percent of Americans saying it is acceptable for themselves or others. Americans also view casinos as engines of economic development and sources of state and local tax revenue, and gambling as a matter of personal choice. Clearly, this trend isn't going to disappear anytime soon.

Where are people gambling most? More than half (51 percent) of all Americans played the lottery in 2006, while fewer than one third (31 percent) participated in casino gambling.

The West continued to generate the largest percentage of casino visitors in 2006, accounting for 33 percent of visitors. However, its share decreased slightly from 2005 levels, while both the Northeast and South saw an increase in the share of visitors they generated. While the north-central region saw a slight decrease of 1 percent, it still accounted for a larger share of casino visitors than either the southern or northeastern regions.

Consumer spending on poker continued to increase in 2006. The growth, while significant, was not as large as it had been over the previous two years. In Nevada and New Jersey—the two largest commercial gaming states—casino visitors spent $238.1 million on organized poker in 2006, a 15 percent increase over 2005 figures.

In Nevada, the only commercial casino state that operates sports books, Americans wagered more than $2.4 billion on sports in 2006, a 7.6 percent increase over 2005. Despite this significant figure, the revenues earned from sports books actually are quite low. In 2006, the gross gaming revenue from Nevada's sports books was $192 million, only 8 percent of the amount wagered.

Accounting for almost half of the total amount bet, football was the most popular sport on which to wager in the Nevada sports books in 2006. Each year, more bets are placed on the Super Bowl than on any other sporting event. The amount wagered on the game and casino gross revenues fluctuate each year due to the result of the game and the point spread. In 2007, more than $93 million was wagered on the game, yielding $12.9 million in revenue, nearly 14 percent of the amount bet.

WHO'S GAMBLING?

The income differential between the U.S. population as a whole and U.S. casino customers remains significant, with casino players earning approximately 16 percent more than the average American. In 2006, the typical casino customer was one year older (forty-seven) than the average American, mirroring 2005's age differential. White-collar workers made up 27 percent of casino customers; other workers accounted for 41 percent, retired individuals made up 20 percent, and blue-collar workers represented 13 percent of casino visitors.

Casinos, it is said, function as economic engines in local communities. Of course, wages for gaming-services workers vary according to occupation, level of experience, training, location, and size of the gaming establishment.

MEDIAN EARNINGS FOR GAMING-SERVICES OCCUPATIONS (MAY 2004)

Gaming supervisors	$40,840
Slot-key persons	$23,010
All other gaming service operators	$20,820
Gaming and sports books writers and runners	$18,390
Gaming dealers	$14,340

INTERNET GAMBLING

The online gambling industry has grown steadily over the last decade, resulting in a $14.5 billion market worldwide. Internet gambling revenues are anticipated to climb to $25 billion by the year 2010, nearly half of which is foreseen to come from domestic players, with Japan and China, who gamble twice as much as they shop online, trailing close behind.

There are currently more than two thousand gambling sites on the Internet, and online gambling revenue in the United States was $5.9 billion in 2005. Online gamblers' numbers doubled in 2005 alone. Typically, the U.S. Internet gambler is a young male, under forty and college educated. He's typically more affluent than his fellow citizens. It's estimated that 4 percent of the U.S. population gambled online in 2005, and more than $200 million is bet daily on Internet poker. Moreover, the 2006 enactment of antigambling laws certainly isn't doing much to slow the industry's astounding rate of growth. Only 19 percent of U.S. Internet gamblers realize or care that the activity is illegal according to current law.

A current concern regarding this niche industry has to do with a greater degree of addiction. This is simply a result of the fact that Internet gambling sites provide players a higher level of access than the traditional casino. However, gambling odds are often better at online casinos than offline ones, though on certain types of games (like slots), where the odds are set by the casino, online casinos have lower overhead and employ fewer people. Thus, online casinos are able to return more money to online gamblers in the form of winnings while still making a profit.

The key difference between online and offline casinos is that online casinos use software that controls game play using random number generators to ensure fairness. The best online casinos use software from a major provider known to provide quality game play with fair results.

Until recently, U.S. laws governing Internet gambling have been ambiguous, leaving the way open for the online industry to flourish with American customers. But while new legislation now categorically outlaws online gambling (the previous 1961 Wire Act was only used to charge firms that took sports bets), American gamblers will no doubt still find a way to pay their online bets. That's because, despite the new law, the majority of the more than two thousand offshore online gambling companies will continue to take bets from the United States. American gambling resorts and casinos like MGM Mirage and Harrah's Entertainment (which is reportedly being eyed by a private-equity consortium) may be among the few to profit from the new law. Along with the horse-racing industry, lotteries, and fantasy sports operators, they have been exempted from it.

HOW DO WE PLAY THIS?

As always, there's the front door and the backdoor. The front door is to invest directly in all the companies where people do their gambling: the casinos, the racetrack, Las Vegas, Macao, etc. Sometimes these companies could be loaded with debt and stand on shaky ground, however, so, as always, the way to avoid the sand traps is to

find the superinvestors who love the sector and to piggyback them.
They have the track record and the expertise to do better research
than you and I can do.

Here's an example: The Marsico Focus Fund (MFOCX) is a
growth fund run by Thomas Marsico. Now, in a small mutual-fund
company with only one or two funds, it's not unusual for the whole
company to have the same name as the guy who is running the fund.
Marsico Capital, however, runs dozens of funds with $10 billion un-
der management, and founder Thomas Marsico chooses to spend his
time running the Marsico Focus Fund, a $5 billion fund with his fa-
vorite picks. The fund is focused primarily on growth stocks and
tends to be a long-term holder.

One of Marsico Focus Fund's largest positions is Las Vegas Sands
(LVS). This company owns casinos in Las Vegas (at the Venetian)
and Macao (at the Sands Macao), and has several other casinos in
development. As of this writing, Marsico has $384 million invested
in LVS.

Is Marsico worth following?

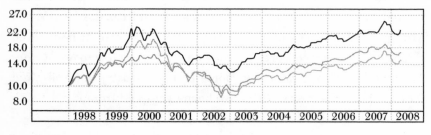

Source: Morningstar

It is up an annualized 9.64 percent over the past ten years
versus 3.73 percent for the S&P 500. And it has consistently outperformed.

But let's not rely solely on Marsico. It's also interesting that a
quality value fund, Thornburg Value Fund (TGVAX), is a shareholder of LVS. Let's look at Thornburg's returns in the same ten-
year period.

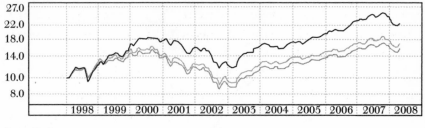

Source: Morningstar

There's an annualized return of 9.58 percent, again steadily out-performing the S&P 500 and its peer group.

This is not directly a recommendation for LVS, but now we know several things:

1. The company is in the gambling sector, and this is going to be a nonstop trend over the next fifty years.
2. LVS is well exposed to the two world centers of gambling: Las Vegas and Macao in the People's Republic of China.
3. Two top investors, a growth investor and a value investor, are significant shareholders of the company.

As a small portion of a forever portfolio, it's not a bad bet. Another company with similar characteristics is MGM, run by Kirk Kerkorian, who is been an investor and entrepreneur in Las Vegas for almost fifty years. The Marsico Focus Fund is also in MGM, as is Private Capital, the value-oriented hedge fund run by superinvestor Bruce Sherman (whose claim to fame is that he's probably held stock in more companies acquired by Buffett's Berkshire Hathaway than any other investor).

Then there's the backdoor—the companies that make the nuts and bolts required for gambling. The king in this space is International Game Technology (IGT). You can't get more nuts-and-bolts in the gambling space than slot machines, and that's exactly what IGT produces. Let's look at IGT's net income. It shows a nice trend over the past nine years.

Year	IGT Revenue (millions)
2007	$508
2006	$473
2005	$436
2004	$429
2003	$375
2002	$254
2001	$213
2000	$156
1999	$65

I like the fact that the recession of 2001 was one of the company's best growth periods ever. I also like that our old friends Private Capital (see MGM above) is one of its largest shareholders.

I also have long been a follower of CryptoLogic (CRYP). This company makes the software used by many of the online poker Web sites. It has recently been subject to the cruel fates imposed by U.S. regulators, but despite that, several value investors have taken a shine to the company, and I expect it to ride out any pain and be a long-term gainer over the next few decades. Mohnish Pabrai, one of my favorite value investors to follow, is a large investor in CRYP.

14

How to Be a Great Man and Learn from Great Men

I'm afraid I'm never going to be a great man. Here's why: I was talking to an analyst at one of the top two banks the other day, and he was describing to me why a particular CEO was great and hence his company was a potential buy. "He even flies coach everywhere," the analyst said.

Huh, I thought to myself, this is really not good for me. For instance, if I had only $500 to my name and a coach ticket was $300 but business class was $600, then I would stand on a corner, hat in hand, and beg until I raised the $100 so I could fly business class. It's not that I'm a snob, but I like the extra attention I get for what would be an otherwise miserable five-hour trip, not to mention the extra leg room for my massive five-foot-nine-inch frame.

But why is someone great if he flies coach, particularly if he is the CEO of a company with $10 billion in revenues? If I were a shareholder, I'd want my CEO to be comfortable. Heck, I'd want him to fly a private jet so he could get more work done! Why is it always considered better to be an ascetic?

Here are some other examples of alleged greatness:

"He only makes one dollar a year in salary." This includes heavy hitters like Sergey Brin, Larry Page, Steve Jobs, and Richard Kinder at Kinder Morgan. All of these guys might be great (Richard Kinder in particular), but trust me, they make billions in every other way, so raising their yearly salary to $100,000 wouldn't make a dent in profits.

"He answers his own phone." The other day, a friend of mine called Charlie Munger, Warren Buffett's right-hand man, the vice-chairman of Berkshire Hathaway. Munger picked up his own phone. That's incredible. He picked it up with his own hands. People are lucky if I even return their messages a week later, let alone pick up the phone.

"He doesn't give earnings guidance." Great men can't give guidance. Buffett doesn't do it. Page and Brin don't do it. Microsoft gives guidance, but for fifteen years people haven't picked up on the fact that it always downplays the next year as not as good as the last. Buffett does that also. This is called underpromising and overdelivering, and it's an incredibly useful skill if you can do it. Unfortunately, I can't do it. I tend to overpromise and then have to work extra hard to overdeliver.

"He's a straight shooter." Check out the 8-K filings for Expeditors International. The CEO, Peter Rose, publishes a Q & A he does with analysts, and he is brutal. If an analyst asks a dumb question, it will be plastered all over that 8-K filing for everyone to read. Still, Expeditors's 8-K filings are filled with greatness. In the last one, someone asked why the company doesn't buy back more shares. In the third paragraph of his answer, Rose said, "We are not ignorant of the theory of how increasing financial leverage results in maximizing returns. That having been said, over the years, we've seen repeated examples of others in this business who've fallen under the spell of erudite consultants and investment bankers, all using the right buzz-words espousing the benefits of some financial transaction, buttressed by financial theories that in reality only supported what we call 'the clandestine rule of finance.' Once in their clutches, these erstwhile competitors got talked into doing things that in finance textbooks made perfect sense, but in the real world had catastrophic effects on their business. Yogi Berra never went to Harvard Business School, but he did understand one important principle. As he said, 'In theory, there is no difference between theory and practice. In practice, there is.' "

Other examples of greatness: still driving the Buick you were conceived in the back seat of. Still living in an apartment you share with five roommates and two dogs. Scheduling all of your own appointments. Eating only what you grow yourself. And so on.

Now, this list may seem a little snarky, as if I don't believe these men truly are great and I'm making fun of them a bit. But actually I do believe they're great. I wish I were like any of the above CEOs, with any of the above attributes. They're admirable, and I like all of their companies and all of their stocks. Heck, I wrote a book on Buffett. Brin and Page have taken a unified philosophy of "technology plus customer satisfaction" to create the greatest company in the world. Kinder left assetless Enron to build the best pipeline company in the world, which he's now taking private. Jobs changed my life by allowing me to watch *Desperate Housewives* on the train every day. I'd been waiting for something like that since 1978, and on a dollar-a-year salary, he was able to finally do it. And if you want a textbook study of how to run a public company, the Expeditors 8-Ks (next to Buffett's straight-shooting annual letters and any talk given by Munger) are must-reads.

Yes, I wish I were as great as these CEOs. But I'm not. I can still emulate their business acumen through my investments, however, and you can too.

GET MENTORS WHOM YOU REMEMBER FOREVER

I try to learn from everybody I can, and I've had many mentors—at least a dozen—in my life. Unfortunately, people who have great wisdom often also have great flaws, and you may have to carefully sort through the dark coal to find the real gems. This is the roller-coaster ride that happens on the way to acquiring wisdom. You can't obtain knowledge without experiencing many painful moments that, through trial and error, you learn to work your way through. I'll give you an example that is somewhat sad.

In 1998, I wanted to sell a company I had started. I found a buyer, and the guy in the middle was named Shlomo (not his real name, but close). The deal was for stock, and before the deal closed, the stock price had moved up considerably, making the value of the deal much higher for me. You would think this would be a source of joy, but it was the opposite. I was miserable every time that stock went higher, because I felt for sure the buyer would back out or try to lower the price, that he would resent the amount of money I would be making on the deal. I almost even made the fatal mistake of negotiating against myself by offering to lower the price before they asked.

Finally I called Shlomo and explained my concern. He told me, "Listen, I only worry about what's in *my* pocket. I don't worry about what's in *your* pocket." Not only did that one (perhaps obvious) line put me at ease, but I've also repeated it to myself on many occasions since then when I found myself resenting, or even jealous about, the amounts of money people were making on various deals I was involved in. Jealousy is a natural emotion. But repeating that one phrase kept me, in almost Zen-like fashion, focused on myself and my own needs and desires, as opposed to what others were making or feeling.

Another Shlomo moment: We were looking to buy a certain company after the deal on my company finally closed. We visited another Internet services firm. Shlomo, at the beginning of the meeting, said, "I don't know the Internet from a hamburger, but everyone here will make a lot of money if we do this deal." He wasn't overly focused on any one business sector; rather, he was an opportunist and was willing to dive into any sector or idea that would make him money. He was also a strong momentum-trend follower. In fact, during the Internet bust, and after 9/11, he ended up making quite a bit of money on a terrorist-defense play.

This was all before everything came to an end, and here's where the story changes, not only for Shlomo, but for everyone who knew him. It turned out that about twenty years earlier, among his many other business efforts, he set up a currency brokerage firm with a bunch of other people. Investors would give them money to buy and sell currencies, like a stockbroker, but with currencies instead of stocks. The only catch was that Shlomo and his buddies would take the money and put it in their pockets and forge account statements. I don't know all the details, but eventually the FBI caught on and a massive sting resulted. Shlomo and his whole crew are in jail now. I never spoke to him again after I read about it in the paper.

So does that make all his advice bad? Clearly he has done evil, and there is no excuse for his stealing millions of dollars from investors. But he always dealt with me fairly, and I learned many things from him. The whole incident disturbed me greatly, and I thought that clearly he was a tortured soul. Or was he? I don't know. But I learned something, somehow.

Another mentor is a hedge-fund manager I used to trade for. This guy's personality is somewhat larger than life, and he's notorious for completely blowing up his hedge fund time and time again, although he always manages to get a second, third, and fourth chance. In many ways, he treated me very poorly, but I learned one important thing from him that made me a lot of money.

At one point in his career he was in the business of selling businesses. He would broker deals. He told me that when he had a business to sell, he would get the names and addresses of twenty potential buyers in the space. He would contact each of them with the details of the business he was selling. Maybe six would respond. Then there would be three serious visits and potential offers, and finally one offer and deal closing. It was the 20-6-3-1 rule, as I later termed it. Since then, I've been involved in a few businesses that I helped sell. I've always used this rule, and it's always worked. Most recently, the rumor is that this hedge-fund manager completely blew up again with a $380 million fund. In some ways, he simply could not get out of his own way to be a success. But he's been through a lot and has the experience to share.

There are too many others to list, but the common thread of all the advice I received was that it was strikingly simple and clear: You don't need to know advanced physics to see the colors of a rainbow.

15

Piggybacking

Whenever Warren Buffett announces he's bought a stock, the stock invariably moves higher that day as people rush in to piggyback the greatest investor ever. However, sometimes you want to ride in an ocean liner, and sometimes you want to ride in a speedboat to get a bit more of the thrill. Buffett might be the greatest investor ever, but there might be other ways to get the Buffett magic touch by piggybacking some of the alternatives I'm about to outline.

Buffett has an unparalleled track record dating back to the 1950s, when he set up his initial investment partnership. In the fifties (as I've documented in the classic tome *Trade Like Warren Buffett*), he was able to trade more frequently and also build positions in his favorite "cigar butt" stocks: small-cap or microcap stocks that were trading for less than their assets and were usually quick hits to Buffett's returns.

Since then, Buffett has built up a cash stockpile of more than $50 billion, and it's harder for him to maneuver around in his positions. The benefit to piggybacking him, then, is that it's unlikely he's going to be an active trader. Once he starts loading up on a position, he sticks with it. For instance, in the summer of 2007, he started loading up on Burlington Northern, a U.S. railroad. Based on his filings, it appears he began buying in the upper $70s, bought some more in the $80s, watched it dip to the mid-$70s, and as of the time of this writing, the stock is at $89.

BURLINGTON NORTHERN SANTA FE CORP.
as of May 14, 2008

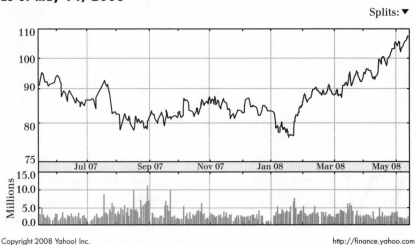

Splits: ▼

Copyright 2008 Yahoo! Inc.   http://finance.yahoo.com

Academic research shows that Buffett is worth piggybacking. In a soon-to-be-released study, Gerald Martin of American University and John Puthenpurackal of the University of Nevada–Las Vegas reach the following conclusion: Buying whatever Warren Buffett bought, often months after his purchases, delivered twice the return of the S&P 500 Index during the past three decades. Investors would have earned an annual 24.6 percent by buying the same stocks as Buffett after he disclosed them in regulatory filings, sometimes even four months later. The S&P rose 12.8 percent a year during the same period.

However, because of Buffett's sheer size, he has other considerations than those of the average investor. He's extremely long-term in his approach, looking mostly for large demographic trends that could take decades to play out. He's also not interested in smaller, undervalued situations, because they won't move the needle on his enormous stockpile of cash.

Through most of this book, I also recommend looking at the large demographic trends. This approach was inspired, in part, by the research I did for my book on Buffett. I like the idea of getting a portfolio that I never visit again. However, I do think it's worth looking regularly at the portfolios of value investors and activist investors to see what ideas they are coming up with, what stocks look cheap, and what trends might be appearing.

Value investors tend to buy situations that are cheap relative to their assets. An extreme example is if a stock is trading for a market cap lower than the value of the cash they have in the bank. Don't laugh. That happened quite a bit in the crash of 2000–02, but it doesn't happen as frequently now. Activist investors tend to buy into situations where they think the company is not only undervalued but also poorly managed. They then use their share holdings in the company to try to influence management. I will have more on these guys below and how we can piggyback them, but I want to address Warren Buffett first. I like Buffett, but it's almost old news whenever he announces he's in a stock. Everyone rushes into it. Dozens of articles come out about the stock (often including ones written by me), and the stock starts to trade based on whether or not people think Buffett will add to his position. But I like to look at four other possible ways to piggyback a Buffett-like approach.

1. YOU NEED TO KNOW HIS STOCKBROKER

When Buffett was moving up in the investment world in the 1960s and early 1970s, he used Tweedy Browne as his brokerage firm. For instance, Tweedy Browne helped him accumulate much of his stake in the (at the time) microcap Berkshire Hathaway (BRKA).

Tweedy Browne was founded by several former employees of the investment firm Graham-Newman, which was renowned investor Benjamin Graham's company. They went on to form the very successful Tweedy Browne Global Value Fund. Last year the fund was up 20.1 percent, and its three-year annualized return is 17.5 percent. Chris Browne recently wrote *The Little Book of Value Investing* with Tim Melvin, a good friend of mine and an excellent trader.

In its Q4 2006 letter to investors, Chris Browne said, "It seems the world has been awash in a sea of liquidity caused at least in part by an abundance of low cost credit. This unprecedented level of free flowing cash has stimulated demand for virtually all financial asset classes. . . . In general, as value investors, we tend to add the most value when we are being well compensated for the risks we are bearing. This is not one of those times. Global equities, for the most part, are pretty fully valued. While we are still uncovering deeply undervalued equities from time to time and cash reserve levels have receded somewhat in both of our Funds, bargains still remain scarce."

Given that level of skepticism about the markets in general, it's interesting to review periodically what some of their long-term holdings are, particularly for a forever portfolio.

ILLINOIS TOOL WORKS
as of May 14, 2008

One of the possibilities is Illinois Tool Works (ITW). Primarily I like this company just for the name. The company makes metal and plastic fasteners for the commercial and residential construction industries. In other words, this is a backdoor play on housing and might not get as hurt if there are any temporary gluts of unsold inventory. It's interesting to see Buffett buying companies like USG (USG)—which makes furnishings for the housing industry—and Tweedy Browne buying ITW, which is a bit lower on the supply chain of the housing industry. While housing might have a temporary blip in its history, that blip won't last forever. And regardless of the direction of housing prices, eventually people will need to build homes. The U.S. and world populations are only getting bigger. The extra billion people who will inhabit the planet (and the additional 50 million people who will inhabit the United States) twenty years from now will all need a place to live. While housing seems like a scary trend to bet on in the summer of 2008, for the long term, there's not really a safer industry.

Also, as of early 2008, Tweedy Browne has been adding to their positions in SK Telekom (SKM), the largest Korean telecom provider. This can be seen as a backdoor way of playing China and the growth in the Asian economies. Why not buy directly into China? You can do that, but there's risk while China is still figuring out its regulatory issues, dealing with the transition from communism to capitalism, etc., whereas the Korean economy, while capitalist, is one of the largest exporters to China and is directly linked to the success of the Chinese economy. Buying a company that services the needs of Korean businesses (regardless of how China does) but will certainly do better as China does better, and also trades at 10 times cash flows, is probably a good way to bet on China.

SK TELECOM ADR
as of Feb. 15, 2008

Splits: ▼

Copyright 2008 Yahoo! Inc.   http://finance.yahoo.com

2. YOU NEED TO LOOK FOR THE NEXT BERKSHIRE HATHAWAY

You might not find stocks that go from $10 (where Buffett started buying his shares) to $100,000, but it's not so bad if you can find stocks that go from $400 to $100,000—as many Berkshire millionaires were able to do. In my earlier book, I tell the story of a guy I met at the 2003 annual meeting who bought two hundred shares of BRKA in 1976 when they were trading around $100. He sold one hundred of his shares when the stock doubled, figuring he'd lock in some gains. The hundred shares he held on to are now worth $14 million. Think about that.

I think it's a good idea to look for companies that could be the next Berkshire Hathaway, i.e., like the way Buffett ran Berkshire over the past several decades. It's also good to look at the stocks these companies own.

First is Markel (MKL), a niche insurance company that focuses on specialty markets. It is somewhat similar to Berkshire Hathaway, although on a much smaller scale. Markel has a $4 billion market cap versus Berkshire's $160 billion market cap.

Before I explain why Markel is a great company, worthy of Berkshire's attentions as a suitor, it's worth giving a brief overview of how an insurance company works. Basically, insurance companies take in money (premiums) and invest it, fervently hoping that they can increase it before their customers want their money back. Why would they want the money back? They don't really—that's the beauty of the industry. But if a customer of an auto insurance company, for instance, gets into a car accident, then the insurance company owes money to that customer.

The *float* is basically the premium. (That's a simplified definition but good enough for our purposes.) Most insurance companies lose a little money on their float—anywhere from 0 percent to 10 percent is common—meaning they pay out more than they take in from customers but make money on their investments. Berkshire Hathaway often does the remarkable, making money on its float, too.

Markel's cost of float, like Berkshire's, is negative. In other words, it makes good money on its float. And it makes even better money on its investments. Year over year, in mid-2007, its investments were up 13 percent, and its year-over-year overall change in net income was 28.8 percent.

Markel's net investment income is driven by Tom Gayner, its chief investment officer. At forty-five years old, Gayner has a couple of decades' experience but a few decades left to go in his career. On the company's latest earnings call, he reiterated his belief that today's market is cheap relative to valuations in prior decades, and he likes companies that are growing their earnings by double digits and that have great returns on equity.

He also likes drug companies paying high dividends, as well as companies with heavy exposure to foreign countries, in particular those focused on Brazil, Russia, India, and China—the so-called BRIC bloc.

The second name I believe should be on Buffett's radar is Brookfield Asset Management (BAM). This company, which has about $50 billion in assets under management, has a real-estate division, an investment division, and even a power/utility division, under which it operates everything from hydroelectric power facilities to wind-power companies. Brookfield also runs private equity funds, mutual funds, and income funds.

While I'm not a technical analyst, it's hard not to notice and appreciate the long-term picture of this stock's chart. That straight line up is a reflection of the company's financials. Revenue grew 66 percent in the fourth quarter of 2006 versus the same quarter in the prior year. Operating cash flow over the last year grew 35 percent, and in 2005 it grew 45 percent.

BROOKFIELD ASSET
as of May 14, 2008

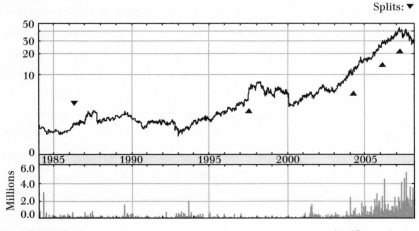

Cash flow comes from all of the company's disparate properties, ranging from its office buildings to its power facilities, its collection of timberland as well as its investments and the fees it charges on money it takes in from outside investors. CEO John Flatt focuses on long-term investments and looks for companies that can sustain annual growth of 12 percent or more in cash flows.

One of the best value investors ever, Marty Whitman, who runs the Third Avenue Value Fund, is a long-term Brookfield shareholder. Whitman is up 19.22 percent on average over the past three years. So it's helpful to know that other great investors are piggybacking BAM.

3. YOU NEED TO KNOW HIS FRIENDS

Bill Ruane set up the Sequoia Fund. Ruane passed away in 2005, but his fund lives on. When Buffett shut down his hedge fund in 1970, he suggested to his investors that they put their money in Sequoia. Ruane and his partner had started the firm specifically to handle Buffett's investors. Since 1970, Sequoia has had an annualized return of 15.7 percent.

Of course, Berkshire Hathaway is on the list of Sequoia's positions. Sequoia has also been a long-term shareholder of MasterCard (MA) and various retailers, including Best Buy (BBY).

It's also worthwhile to watch another Buffett friend and Berkshire board member, Bill Gates. Gates is a semisuccessful software programmer who got interested in investing after playing bridge online for many hours a day with the young Warren Buffett. I used to think that Gates was heavily influenced by Buffett, but now I'm starting to wonder if it's the other way around. For instance, although Buffett has been buying up shares of railroads throughout 2007, he attributes his interest in the sector to Bill Gates showing him the benefits of one of Gates's holdings, Canadian Northern (CNI).

BILL GATES'S HOLDINGS, VIA CASCADE

Ticker	Company Name
CNI	Canadian National Railway (USA)
RSG	Republic Services, Inc.
BRKA	Berkshire Hathaway, Inc.
TV	Grupo Televisa, S.A. (ADR)
PNM	PNM Resources, Inc.
OTTR	Otter Tail Corp.
WIW	Western Asset Claymore U.S. Treasury Inflation Protected Securities Fund 2
SIX	Six Flags, Inc.
WIA	Western Asset Claymore U.S. Treasury Inflation Protected Securities Fund
FSCI	Fisher Communications, Inc.
LGBT	PlanetOut, Inc.
PEIX	Pacific Ethanol, Inc.

4. YOU NEED TO SHADOW THE VALUE INVESTORS

In addition to the investors mentioned above, throughout this book I've referred to other value investors who are invested in companies that we're looking at for a forever portfolio. Despite the fact that there's always a legal disclaimer for mutual funds and hedge funds, "past performance is not indicative of future performance," I don't quite believe this. I do think that value investors, who consistently look for undervalued stocks, tend to outperform others over time.

Furthermore, I like the approach of finding the best value and activist investors, looking up their positions, and piggybacking the ones that correspond with other trends described in this book. Every investor with more than $100 million in stock holdings is required to list their holdings each quarter in a 13F-HR filing with the SEC.

The filing comes forty-five days after the end of the quarter so, one can argue, the filings are out of date. But investors like Carl Icahn or Warren Buffett are unlikely to be doing much selling of their long-term positions. There are many investors like them, who rarely trade in and out of positions but tend to hold for the long run. Via Stockpickr.com, a site I set up with my business partner, Dan Kelly, in 2006, we have done a study of who those investors are and have set up their portfolios on that site.

CAN INVESTORS AVOID FILING THEIR HOLDINGS WITH THE SEC?

I'm flattered. You would be too if something you wrote was mentioned in a filing with the Securities and Exchange Commission by someone trying to prove his constitutional rights were violated. And particularly as those rights were allegedly violated by me (and others of my ilk) because of Rule 13(f)(2) in the SEC Act of 1934 (back when young bootlegger Joe Kennedy was writing the rules).

Let me back up. I got an e-mail from a friend of mine whose name I don't know. He writes a blog, the Microcap Speculator, and has chosen to remain anonymous. Bloggers resemble superheroes in this respect. Microcap tells me: "You're famous." And he attaches the filing written up by Phil Goldstein, the general partner of Bulldog Investors, a hedge fund that primarily takes activist stances in publicly traded closed-end funds.

Phil last hit the headlines when he won a lawsuit against the SEC that allowed hedge funds not to have to go through the arduous registration process. Now he's at it again, claiming that the SEC rule requiring him to file a 13F-HR filing once a quarter violates his constitutional rights. The 13F-HR filing is filed by any entity with more than $100 million in assets, and involves disclosing all of the entity's stock holdings. The Fifth Amendment of the Constitution states: "[N]or shall private property be taken for public use without just compensation." And Goldstein adds: "The Applicant's equity holdings are trade secrets that are protected by the Taking Clause of the Fifth Amendment." To support his claim, he quotes a chapter, "Trade Like Jeff Berkowitz," from my last book.

Berkowitz was Jim Cramer's right-hand man at Jim's hedge fund, and he now runs the firm, which has been renamed J. L. Berkowitz & Co. Goldstein quotes my article at length, but the main line is: "I like learning from the stock picks and styles of others. . . . Along these lines, I like looking at the 13F-HR." Snap! Guilty!

Goldstein's missive is nineteen pages, and my response to the various cases and examples he cites could fill just as many pages. But I do have three points to make:

1. A hedge fund is often structured as a partnership in which the manager is the general partner and the investors are limited partners. As such, a hedge fund's money, particularly when it is more than $100 million, is not the private property of the manager, but rather the property of potentially hundreds of institutions, pension funds, endowments, and so on, which together make up the partners of the fund. If I were a teacher in New York and the New York State Teachers Fund were an investor, then indirectly I am an investor and very concerned about the state of my investment in an otherwise illiquid vehicle with high fees and zero transparency.

2. The only real tangible benefit of viewing a 13F-HR filing is the knowledge that forty-five days earlier the fund was not (or was) overconcentrated in any one set of positions. You also get to know if there was any style drift or if any of the statements the manager has made about his portfolio differ from what is revealed.

3. Goldstein assumes we can make use of his picks to avoid doing serious research and simply piggyback his positions. However, although I think these filings have a lot of value (that's what this entire chapter is about), I do think that some individual care and research must be taken because of the forty-five-day delay.

There are two takeaways here:

1. The SEC is not going to change this rule any time soon.
2. There's enough value in these filings that a quality hedge-fund manager like Goldstein thinks it's important enough to sue the Department of Justice to avoid disclosing his positions.

There are many benefits to piggybacking better investors:

Thrift. Piggybacking is like investing in the investors' funds without having to pay their fees. True, there's the forty-five-day delay, but again, focus on the guys who are long-term investors.

Knowledge of space. You and I are not going to be as expert in a field (health care, telecom, etc.) as a sector-specific fund that hires a team of analysts to study and determine the best companies in a space. Piggybacking the experts is a good way to study and invest in a complicated sector.

Thrift, part 2. If Buffett buys BNI at $80 and it goes down to $75, well, who will argue with getting a Buffett pick at a discount?

Diversification. You can diversify across thirty different value investors.

A great employee. It's as if the investor is on our full-time staff for nothing and we can fire him at any time. The investor being piggy-backed:

- Conducts extensive due diligence before entering a position;
- Does proxy battles, hires lawyers, communicates with the management team; and
- We can "fire" the investor anytime we want by selling the position.

Liquidity. Piggybacking makes it easier to enter and exit positions. When Warren Buffett buys $1 billion worth of a stock, it's not so easy to get rid of it. We'll never have that problem (well, maybe we will, but then that's a pleasant problem). For us, there are no filings necessary, we're not fighting management, and we're not tied to any battle.

HOW GOOD ARE THEY?

How good are the activist investors, the ones who seek change in the management of the companies they invest in? In a study out of Northeastern University, "Hedge Funds as Shareholder Activists from 1994–2005," by Nicole Boyson and Robert Mooradian, the authors demonstrate that activist hedge funds actually do accompany improved business performance. They make several points.

- "For our sample, on average both short-term and long-term target performance improves following hedge fund activist activity."
- "In addition, hedge funds themselves are different from other types of activists. First, hedge funds rarely have conflicts of interest (such as politically-motivated agendas) common among pension funds and mutual funds. Second, hedge funds are willing to spend money; the average target firm holding in our sample is about $18 million. Third, although hedge funds are often considered to be short-term investors, this is not true for our sample of activist funds, as the hedge funds typically stay active in their targets for over two years. Fourth, many activist hedge funds have lockup provisions. A lockup provision requires that hedge fund investors not withdraw their money for a fixed time (usually six months to one year), thus encouraging longer term strategies."
- The study also says that the hedge funds' secret weapon might be their ability to own more than 10 percent of a company's stock. Naturally, this makes management take them very seriously.
- What else makes activist funds appear so smart? Regardless whether

they succeed in enacting changes in operational or corporate gover-
nance, they have an ability to identify undervalued targets. A profitable
exit from an activist investment thus may be a self-fulfilling prophecy. According to the authors, the mere presence of an activist hedge fund increases the likelihood of the company being acquired.

It was while Dan Kelly and I were formulating this strategy that
we decided to create Stockpickr.com to allow people to easily peruse
the profiles of the superinvestors. Here's a list of some of the investors we started off with, value or activist investors who tend to be
long-term and look for undervalued stocks, as opposed to doing
momentum-based investing or day trading.

Barington Capital
Shamrock Capital
Steel Partners
Third Point
Chapman Capital
D^3 Family Funds (David Nierenberg)
Icahn Capital
Soros Capital
Pershing Square
ESL Partners (Eddie Lampert)
Renaissance Technologies (mostly short-term traders but with a
    long-only equity fund)
Spencer Capital
Pabrai Investments
Greenlight Capital
Seth Klarman

The list of investors who have quietly and consistently outperformed
the markets for ten years or more is a long one. All of the above tend
to be long-term holders.

Originally, Kelly and I wanted to invest based on the Stockpickr piggybacking approach. A well-known hedge fund with about $10 billion under management liked the idea. They wanted the two of us to trade the strategy with about $100 million, and if it worked out, they would quickly take it up to $200 million or more. But there were various catches. They wanted a 6 percent "cost of capital." In other words, the first 6 percent would have gone to them. They would give us 15 percent of the profits above that. But there's more. They wanted us to "neutralize" every position. So, for instance, if we went long Dendreon then maybe we should short some biotech ETF. Finally, they wanted me to stop all writing. When I ran through the numbers, it was too much risk to take. So we said, screw this, let's just put the entire idea on a Web site, including every other idea we've ever traded with (see the Active Trader section of the site) and open it up to everyone. Make a social network, so to speak. After many discussions with Tom Clarke, CEO of TheStreet.com, and a little-known stock pundit named Jim Cramer, we decided to do this as a joint project, and we launched on January 3, 2007.

Five million unique visitors later, it has definitely worked out well. Currently there are more than a dozen different methods for getting quality stock ideas via the site. I saw from my own writing that what people want more than anything, more than economic commentary, more than sector ideas, more than political insights, is raw stock ideas—in bulk. That's what Stockpickr provides. It's like the financial news with all the news part stripped out. There are eight thousand public companies out there, and the media tend to focus on just twenty of them. Well, about six thousand of those eight thousand will go up over the next year. Stockpickr focuses on those six thousand, because they're what the smartest money managers focus on.

16

Shock-Absorb Your Forever Portfolio
and Avoid the Sidewalks

On October 29, 1929, my grandfather was working on the floor of the New York Stock Exchange. "They told us to walk in the street instead of the sidewalk if we walked out-side," he told me. "People were throwing themselves out of windows." He had cataracts, and I couldn't see his eyes through his dark glasses while he reminisced about the past. "There were so many orders coming onto the floor that we couldn't handle all the paper-work. They had to put us up in the Chelsea Hotel on Twenty-third Street, and we worked all night finishing all the work. We destroyed the room in a huge pillow fight." He was telling me this in 1995, because I was about to move into the Chelsea for what turned into a three-year stay.

"James," my grandmother interrupted, "don't tell them that at the Chelsea. Maybe they'll charge you for what he did." .

It was perfectly natural to think that almost seventy years later, under new management, in the building where Sid killed Nancy, where Dylan Thomas died, drunk in his own vomit, in the lobby, where Madonna wrote her *Sex* book, that I would be somehow charged for an incident decades earlier that my grandfather was involved in on the worst day in U.S. stock-market history.

That's what people do: They worry about things. They remember things that made them feel ugly and scared. And when an "Asian Contagion" hits in 1997 or a dot-com bust happens in 2000, it's no wonder that the echoes of that can be heard in the market's whispers whenever volatility soars 50 percent in a day.

So let's forget about the market. Whenever the Dow falls to lows, remember this: sooner, rather than later, it's going to hit new highs again. I can quote stats, but one image is worth a thousand statistics. Forget about this middling volatility on the way from here to there. The key is to shock-absorb your portfolio by following the experts and keeping track of history.

DOW JONES INDUSTRIAL AVERAGE

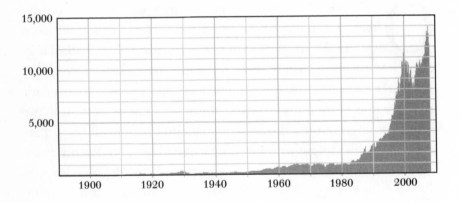

HOW TO SHOCK-ABSORB YOUR PORTFOLIO FOR ALL DISASTERS

One thing I don't really address in this book is wars and geopolitical disasters in general. Yes, there will always be wars on this planet. And investing in defense companies is seldom a bad idea.

But the viability of defense as an investment seems to cycle with political movements as opposed to strong demographic trends. Also, even though we know there are always going to be wars and perhaps other terrorist-led disasters, there's one thing we know for sure: Buy the dips.

Fortunately, there is some history to guide us. Although every situation is different, when disaster strikes, it always appears as if the world is ending or at least that a new era of despair has begun. The day Germany invaded Poland, on September 1, 1939, the S&P was at 11.19. The market took a little dip but then became resilient and closed one week later at 12.69.

When North Korea invaded South Korea in 1950, the S&P 500 fell from 19.14 to 18.11 the day after the invasion and reached a low point of 17.27 one month later. Six months later, however, the S&P 500 was at 21.03.

PRICE HISTORY—S&P 500 INDEX
(5/19/1950-9/12/1950)

Copyright 2008 Yahoo! Inc.   http://finance.yahoo.com

On October 22, 1962, when President Kennedy announced that there were nukes in Cuba, the S&P fell from 55.59 to 53.49 by day's end. One week later, the market was at 55.72, and six months later it was at 70.14, beginning a bull market that would last seven years and never look back.

PRICE HISTORY—S&P 500 INDEX
(9/18/1962-11/20/1962)

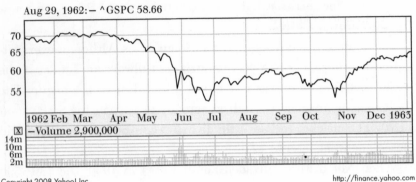

Aug 29, 1962: − ^GSPC 58.66

Copyright 2008 Yahoo! Inc.   http://finance.yahoo.com

Kennedy's assassination in 1963 was another pivotal moment for the markets. Everyone who was alive then can remember exactly where they were when they heard about it. Many were scared for the nation's safety, and the markets momentarily plunged. But look at the chart of what happened (page 167).

The two most dire situations, as far as the market was concerned, were the bombing of Pearl Harbor in 1941 and the Arab oil embargo in 1973. Pearl Harbor took us down 4 percent the day it happened, and it was several years before the market fully recovered. The oil embargo was announced on October 19, 1973. The market was 3 percent lower the next day and then 17 percent lower six months later. However, the oil embargo itself wasn't enough to take the markets down. The week after the embargo was announced, the market was actually 2 percent higher than the close on the day before the embargo was announced.

PRICE HISTORY—S&P 500 INDEX
(10/22/1963-12/24/1963)

Nov 13, 1963: — ^GSPC 73.29

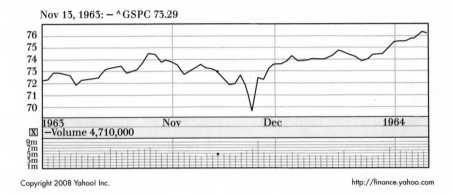

Shocks to the geopolitical situation, on their own, throw the market off temporarily, but not enough to stop the perpetual wheel of industry. Time and time again, the world's markets have rebounded from horrible and tragic situations. After 9/11, the S&P 500 fell from 1092 on September 10, 2001, to a panic-driven low of 944 the week after the disaster. But six months later, despite a war in Afghanistan, Enron's bankruptcy, and the stirrings of trouble at Tyco and WorldCom, the market closed at 1165 on March 18, 2002 (see page 168). At this time, at a historic bottom for real-estate prices, I even managed to sell my apartment in TriBeCa, right next to where the World Trade Center stood.

So whenever there's a disaster, remember this tactic: Wait a week, then buy QQQQ (the proxy ETF for the Nasdaq 100) and SPY (the proxy ETF for the S&P 500). Get the benefits of the resilience of the U.S. economy. Don't worry about making all the money back in one day, but know with confidence that the markets *will* bounce back.

PRICE HISTORY—S&P 500 INDEX
(8/8/2001-1/22/2002)

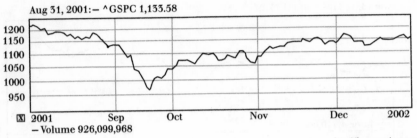

Aug 31, 2001:– ^GSPC 1,133.58

http://finance.yahoo.com

17

The Entire Internet Is Going Down and There's Nothing We Can Do

bout eleven years ago, a friend of mine was pitching a TV show to various networks. The entire premise of his show was that he was going to play practical jokes on MTV. For instance, he called up the producers of the show *The MTV Beach House* and told them his little brother was "afflicted" and had made a wish to visit the show's beach house. "What's wrong with him?" the producer asked. "He's afflicted," my devious friend replied. He would then do everything: Plane tickets would be arranged, bands would be booked, etc. Hilarity would ensue when the truth was discovered. It wasn't my favorite idea of his, but he was set on pursuing it. So I decided to play a trick on my friend.

MTV.com's e-mail system had some unfortunate security issues at the time. I logged into the backdoor there and sent my friend an e-mail from legal@mtv.com informing him he was in serious trouble and MTV was going to take every "litigious and federal" action at its disposal. My friend panicked and left repeated apologies at the network's legal office until I calmed him down and told him what I had done. We're not really friends anymore, but I wave hi when I see him across the street.

Note to MTV: This was the only time I did this. I never showed anyone else how to do it. And, to your credit, you patched the hole about a year later. Also, I'm assuming there's some sort of hacking statute of limitations on this sort of thing. So don't mess with me.

You would think, eleven years and tens of billions of dollars later, that things would be better from a security point of view. But they aren't. They are far worse than anyone realizes. If you buy a computer at the store, take it out of the box, and plug it into your cable modem without any sort of firewall, it will probably be infected within thirty minutes. And once this happens, you might as well throw it out or at least wipe the hard drive clean, because there's nothing you can do about it. What will it be infected with? One of those viruses that Norton AntiVirus can take care of? No, that's old-school (see chapter 2).

The new-school viruses are the so-called bot armies. A *bot* is a piece of software that attaches itself to the lowest levels of your computer and simply does nothing. It's like a sleeper cell, and it can sit there dormant for years. Every now and then, it will wake up to do two things: It will head out to various Internet chat rooms to see if the "botmaster" has left instructions for it. The other thing a bot will do is rewrite itself, so if any antivirus software was created to try to find it, the search will fail—the bot will have morphed into something else. It's literally a cancer that can't be found or stopped, and nobody knows how many bot armies are out roving.

About 50 million computers worldwide, including computers in about half of the S&P 500, are infected with these bots right now. What do these bots do when they are given an assignment? Often they become spam gateways and quietly send out millions of spam e-mails without the owner of the computer realizing. Other times they're used to launch denial-of-service attacks against companies or large Web sites. Or they are used to keep track of all credit-card numbers entered on the computer, which are then gathered by the botmaster and sold onto the identity-theft black market. It's no longer twelve-year-old Russian kids writing these types of malware. Those twelve-year-olds are now nineteen-year-old kids being paid by various criminal organizations to build ever more sophisticated bot armies. In 2007, when I was visiting an antibot startup made up of PhD programmers, I asked them, "What happens when the guys making these bots get as smart as you guys?" They started laughing and replied, "They're much smarter than us already." The common refrain now when I talk to any programmer in the security industry is, "Why haven't they brought the Internet down yet? It would be trivial and there's nothing we can do about it. The bots could just get the command to shut down and wipe out everything on every computer they infect."

Fortunately, from a forever portfolio perspective, there might be ways to play this potential disaster. Forget the security software companies. They might be useless for this particular problem (although still important for the problems mentioned in chapter 2). The hardware guys, Cisco (CSCO) and Juniper (JNPR), are buying companies in the space and developing hardware to detect these intruders at the network level. They are probably good purchases here. But the only real way to avoid getting infected is to never put anything on your computer. Always store things remotely. Only one company provides the services and software to allow this at an enterprise level: VMware (VMW).

VMware provides virtualization software that makes it appear everything is on your computer, when in reality all your files are instead on hard drives in its corporate data center. This allows companies much more thorough protection against these bots, as well as significant saving on IT maintenance costs. I'm not the only one who thinks VMware is a home run: Intel and Cisco are long-term investors in the company, and Hewlett-Packard and IBM (competitors to EMC) are among VMware's largest customers. This company will be around fifty years from now.

Is all hope lost? Eventually will the entire Internet go down and hard drives get wiped out around the world? Probably. But think back to what it was like pre-Internet, take a deep breath, and make sure you still remember how to enjoy a good sunset. They can't take that away from you.

18

Patents Make the World Go 'Round

The hard part in investing, let alone in constructing a portfolio that one hopes will withstand the test of time fifty years out, is that so many factors that are almost impossible to predict can affect the future of a company. Yet it's sometimes easier to predict longer-term events than specific short-term events. For instance, I know with 100 percent certainty that fifty years from now, July will be one of the three hottest months of the year in the United States. But I have no idea what next Tuesday's weather might bring.

Likewise, one problem I have in coming up with companies to consider is that we know a lot of facts about these companies right now, but we really have no idea where they will be fifty years from now. For instance, a company might have a lot of cash, no debt, great investors, and a low P/E ratio at the moment, but all of that could change significantly over time. Ineffective management, changing product lines, or increased competition could alter all of these factors. From an investment perspective, there are several ways we mitigate this risk, which is what this book is all about.

- **Find companies that are focused on large demographic trends.** For instance, if a company is focused on distributing cures for monitoring a side effect of obesity (a demographic trend that is not going away), such as sleep apnea, then chances are that company will continue to grow for the foreseeable future unless it inexplicably decides to shut down its fastest-growing division. Some people are afraid of success, so I suppose it's possible.
- **Find companies with good "buy and hold" investors in them.** Warren Buffett has often said that his "favorite holding period is forever." I don't always believe this of him, but that's the type of investor I try to follow. If several of them are in a stock, it's a sign that they view the company as a long-term hold based on demographic trends.
- **Find companies that have hidden, long-term assets that aren't going away.** Cash is a very visible long-term asset but can easily disappear. Real-estate holdings can be hidden on balance sheets or recorded there, and they are a little harder to "spend." For a few years in the early 2000s, after Eddie Lampert, one of the most successful hedge-fund managers ever, so successfully monetized his real-estate holdings in Sears and Kmart, it became all the rage to look for undervalued real-estate assets, particularly when real-estate prices were skyrocketing more than 20 percent a year.

It's this third area that this chapter is about, but I'll tie in the other two areas as well.

In particular, the hidden assets that I'm interested in are patents. Let's say you own a company. There are several types of assets your business could have. I'm not talking necessarily about strictly defined balance-sheet assets, but rather what any entrepreneur would like to have in his hand as he's starting his company, as well as the sorts of things investors (or acquirers) look for when evaluating a company: cash, customers, tangible property, and intellectual property.

Cash was mentioned above.

Customer contracts are not necessarily long-term assets (depending on the length of the contracts), but they are a good sign that future cash flows for the length of the contract are somewhat stable, assuming you're able to collect on receivables. Customer contracts are perhaps the most important items looked at when a potential acquirer is conducting its due diligence. The contracts prove the viability of any claims about long-term cash flows, growth, and so forth. Without contracts, all of your customers could disappear.

In the midnineties, for instance, I started and ran an Internet company that built Web sites for Fortune 500 customers, including Con Edison, American Express, Toshiba, HBO, Universal, and BMG. But I was a naive businessman then, and most of my deals were "signed" with a handshake. I had strong personal relationships with each of the customers, and even now, ten years after the business was sold, I still have good relationships with many of them. But when we were looking to sell the company (or even get a credit line from a bank on our receivables), it was very grueling to go through the due diligence process. Instead, an acquiring company had to focus on the asset of people within the firm and decide whether or not these people (e.g., me) were the equivalent of long-term customer contracts. If you have people on staff with strong technological, sales, or business-development backgrounds, then this can often be a very significant asset that doesn't appear on the balance sheet.

The problem with this type of asset is that—and this is particularly true of the type of service business I had in the nineties—"all of your assets walk out the door every night." People, therefore, are not necessarily a long-term asset you can bet on for the next fifty years.

Property includes real estate, machinery, computers, and the like. One type of property is often hidden from view and is extremely difficult to value even if it is in plain sight—intellectual property, which can be assessed by the number of patents a company has or the quality of the patents they have. I'll get into some of the finer details of patents below, but first consider this: When a company makes a discovery or an invention, it's probably been associated with some expense (the research and development costs). But how do you value the potential gain in assets that the invention might yield? It's impossible. You won't really know until there are future cash flows that come from that invention. So usually this asset is largely ignored by the investment universe until it starts to demonstrate actual value.

However, when trying to determine which companies might rise to the top over the next fifty years, there is evidence that companies with large, high-quality patent portfolios can be considered to have hidden assets, and that companies trading at a low market cap relative to those assets are probably being unfairly undervalued by the current investing populace. It's these companies that are worth studying, particularly if they overlap other demographic trends mentioned elsewhere in this book, or have long-term investors who have already done the legwork and due diligence proving that these patents/inventions/discoveries have some value most investors are unaware of.

One research study that has attacked this issue is "Are Scientific Indicators of Patent Quality Useful to Investors?" by Mark Hirschey and Vernon Richardson of the University of Kansas. Patent quality is difficult to measure, so researchers are always trying to assign value to a patent based on various heuristics. For instance, if many other patents filed over the next year refer to prior patent X, then this increases the value of X. Or if a patent has a large number of references to other scientific research related to the field the patent is in, this could increase the value of the patent. The conclusion of the Hirschey and Richardson study is that the higher the quality of the patent (tested by several different measures) and the lower the P/E ratio of the company, the higher the correlation to positive future stock prices.

Another academic who has done very valuable research in this area is Baruch Lev at New York University. He shows that by looking at R & D expenditures in different accounting lights (for instance, not necessarily expensing them right away but expensing them over time—capitalizing them) can allow you to better forecast future stock-market performance. In general, the more R & D, the better. (See "On the Informational Usefulness of R&D Capitalization and Amortization" by Lev in 2005.)

There's more evidence that investing in high-quality patent portfolios, relative to the book value of a company, results in better stock-market returns. One company, Ocean Tomo, has come up with an index of three hundred companies based on the following criteria:

- Potential index constituents include all equities trading on major U.S. exchanges that are among the thousand most liquid securities.
- The potential index constituents are then narrowed to a universe of companies that own patents.
- The patent-owning companies are divided into fifty style and size groups with the highest patent-value-to-book-value ratio using Ocean Tomo's Patent Ratings software. Each group contains an approximately equal number of patent-owning companies.
- The stocks in each group are ranked using a 100 percent rules-based methodology that seeks to identify those stocks that offer the greatest patent value opportunities.
- The six highest-ranking stocks in each group are selected (resulting in a total of three hundred stocks) and are weighted by market capitalization.
- The constituent selection process and portfolio rebalance are repeated once per year.

How has this index performed? What would you have today if you had invested in a portfolio of these companies in 1996? (See the following table and figure).

OCEAN TOMO 300 PATENT INDEX AVERAGE ANNUAL TOTAL RETURN VS. S&P 500 INDEX as of Dec. 31, 2006

Year	Ocean Tomo 300 Patent Index	S&P 500 Index
10	11.38 %	8.42 %
5	5.95 %	6.19 %
3	10.17 %	10.44 %
1	13.10 %	15.79 %

Source: Zephyr StyleADVISOR

Look at the solid outperformance of the S&P 500 at the ten-year mark. With an index of any three hundred companies it's extremely difficult to outperform the S&P 500 (there's too much overlap), but by choosing companies based on the other criteria mentioned in the beginning of this chapter and by also focusing on the patent quality of the companies, greater outperformance (or at least, comfort during periods of market volatility) can be gained.

So how do we find out which companies have high-quality patents? The raw approach won't work, at least not for you and me. Sure, we could go to the patent Web site, or use Google patent search. And we could start to pore over, for instance, all of Microsoft's patents and begin figuring out what other patents link to them and how good they are. As an example, try to understand the patent shown on page 179.

It's one of the most valuable patents ever—for the telephone. And the text and graphics in patents today are far more obtuse and difficult to decipher (at least for me). Fortunately, there are several good resources to use when researching which companies have high-quality patents. The Patent Board (http://www.ipiq.com) contains a Patent Scorecard that lists the top companies (according to their own internal research) ranked by patent quality in each industry. For instance, as of January 1, 2008, for Information Technology, the scorecard had:

2 Sheets—Sheet 2.

A. G. BELL.

TELEGRAPHY.

No. 174,465. Patented March 7, 1876.

Fig 6.

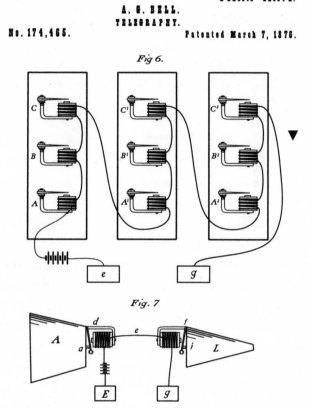

Fig. 7

Witnesses

Ewell A. Dick,
H. J. Hutchinson

Inventor:

A. Graham Bell
by atty. Pollok & Bailey

Rank	Company	Change
1	Microsoft Corp.	▲
2	IBM	▲
3	Hewlett-Packard Co.	—
4	Canon, Inc.	▼
5	Hitachi, Ltd.	▲
6	Ricoh Co., Ltd.	▼
7	Sun Microsystems, Inc.	▲
8	Silverbrook Research Pty., Ltd.	—
9	Xerox Corp.	▼
10	Seiko Epson Corp.	

Compiled with data through Jan. 1, 2008

Or, we can simply go back to our friends at Ocean Tomo. Claymore has put together an ETF of the Ocean Tomo Patent Index (OTP). Again, a sampling of three hundred companies, even ranked by high-quality patents, will be too closely linked to the S&P 500 just by sheer overlap. But we can pick and choose the ones we like by looking at their components and adding in other features.

Here, then, are some of the companies worth studying for a fifty-year portfolio that are also on the Ocean Tomo list of companies with high-quality patents and a low ratio of price to book value.

One company on the Ocean Tomo Patent 300 list, Autoliv (ALV), is the leading beneficiary of a morbid global trend, the rising number of deaths each year from automobile accidents. Approximately a million people died last year from automobile-related accidents, according to the World Health Organization. Because of a theme mentioned throughout this book—the movement of people from rural regions to urban regions in the developing world—that number is expected to continue rising. Companies involved in the development and distribution of products to increase auto safety have a clear path in front of them, regardless of the overall state of the economy, the automobile industry, or any one region's troubles in the auto industry.

Autoliv has about a 30 percent market share in the field of automobile safety, with products like air bags, seat belts, and other safety features. The company isn't going away: It has eighty subsidiaries in twenty-eight countries and deals with all of the major car manufacturers. Because it has operations all over the world, it's easy for Autoliv, over time, to always switch to lower-cost regions such as (for now) Mexico and China. While dividends are something that can change at any moment, the company tends to distribute most of its earnings via dividends and has increased dividends for the past six straight years, currently yielding about 3.2 percent.

AUTOLIV, INC.
as of Apr. 24, 2008

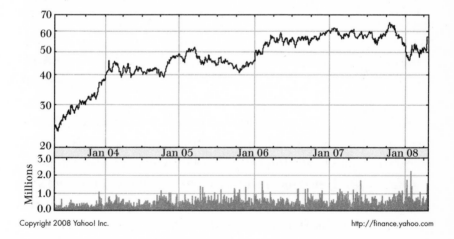

One of the largest shareholders, with $215 million of the stock, is Renaissance Technologies, a hedge fund mentioned throughout this book. Furthermore, a search at the U.S. Patent Office shows Autoliv owning 617 patents. The last three are:

7,328,915:   Airbag cushion with tether deactivated venting for reduced out-of-position effects

7,325,827:   Instrument panel for a motor vehicle having an airbag device integrated in a ventilation arrangement

7,322,595:   Electrically insulated fixing device for an airbag module

SANOFI-AVENTIS, ADS
as of Apr. 24, 2008

As I write this, Warren Buffett has just released in a filing that he recently acquired $162 million worth of Sanofi-Aventis (SNY). SNY appears on the Ocean Tomo Patent 300 index and also intersects nicely with this book's focus on vaccine-development companies (see chapter 3), although it really is a general pharmaceutical company with developments in thousands of health-care products. Again, investing in any company requires an accumulation of small advantages. Health care is a great play due to the aging Baby Boomer demographic, but simply investing in hospital companies might not do the trick because of obscure Medicare regulations that can be changed at any moment. With Sanofi-Adventis, though, now we have several overlapping trends. A search on the text "Sanofi" at the U.S. Patent Office Web site returns 1,616 results with these last three scintillating patents granted:

7,329,673: Acetylated spiropiperidine derivatives as melanocortin-4 receptor agonists

7,329,664: Substituted (7-pyridyl-4-phenylamino-quinazolin-2-yl)-methanol analogues

7,326,789: Sulfur substituted sulfonylaminocarboxylic acid N-arylamides, their preparation, their use and pharmaceutical preparations comprising them

We can go in, analyze those patents, and try to figure out their effect on future cash flows, or we can accumulate our small advantages here and go on to the next stock. Or play a computer game online, which I think I'll do before writing the next paragraph.

Symantec (SYMC) is another stock that has appeared elsewhere (see chapter 2, on computer security). SYMC counts Bruce Sherman's Private Capital Management among its investors, and Sherman is a well-known value-oriented manager. A search on Symantec shows 839 patents at the U.S. Patent Office. Here are the last four:

7,331,062: Method, computer software, and system for providing end to end security protection of an online transaction

7,330,967: System and method for injecting drivers and setup information into pre-created images for image-based provisioning

7,330,887: Method and system for testing web-based applications

7,330,858: Coordinated distributed logging in a multi-host environment

SYMANTEC CORP.

as of Apr. 24, 2008

Splits: ▼

Looking at a company's patents is almost like peeking at your spouse's diary. You get a deeper understanding of what's going on underneath the hood, and it allows you to have a better sense of what's going to happen in the future.

19

Mistakes Were Made; or,
Accumulate Small Advantages to Live Forever

There were three mistakes. The first mistake occurred at an intersection when I was eighteen and a senior in high school. I was driving my dad's car, and I was daydreaming about something (unfortunately, I'm prone to do that), and I went through a stop sign. My car went right into a station wagon that was already in the intersection. All four fences on the four corners were smashed, the station wagon was destroyed, the guy in the station wagon broke his leg, and I went through the window of the car I was driving but somehow, fortunately for me, ended up without a scratch. I wanted to be hurt, I felt so guilty about it. That was the first mistake.

The second mistake occurred when I was ten (I never said these things would be in order). My grandparents took me to the KayBee Toy & Hobby shop in Brunswick Square Mall. Before we got there, my grandpa told me he'd buy me whatever I wanted. At the floor of the New York Stock Exchange in 1929 he had seen how greed kills—

starting on the inside ending with a self-inflicted gunshot to the head (yes, it's an extreme example).

So I went inside the store while they waited outside. It was November, and I liked football cards at the time. I had a winter coat with holes in both pockets, so I'd pick up a pack of cards, walk down an aisle, and put the pack in my pocket and through the hole so my pockets would be empty but the pack of cards would be in the lining of the coat. In other words, I stole the cards, and I repeated this four or five times. Eventually the store manager came up to me and said, "Sir, come back with me." He had me take my coat off, and he shook it until a pack of cards fell out. "Is that it?" he asked, and I nodded my head yes—and he then shook it some more, and another pack came out. And so on. "What did you do?" my grandfather asked when the manager went to get him. "I would've gotten you anything you wanted." That was the second mistake.

Lots of things happen after childhood that are difficult to navigate: jobs, careers, relationships, investments. The burden of worry we carry when we lay our heads down to sleep is hard to overcome even when everything is going our way. There's always the future to plan for, the past to analyze, and the present to try to interpret. I believe the key to success is to acknowledge the enormous number of difficulties in any path and then figure out ways to minimize the stresses and potential for mistakes. I recently invested in a private business, a suite of applications called Buddy Media, which sits on top of Facebook. (It includes an interesting faux currency called AceBucks.) I hate investing in private companies. I like the constant stimulus of seeing what my investment is worth in the public markets. I ran a VC fund during the dot-com bust and I spent far too much time holding the hands of mediocre CEOs, a situation that was no doubt exacerbated by the fact that I was probably a mediocre VC.

But Buddy Media is run by Michael Lazerow, who built and sold Golf.com to Time Warner. When I started Stockpickr.com, over the course of a breakfast, he gave me some incredible ideas, which I was able to blatantly steal from him and execute. So I knew he was good.

My co-investors in Buddy Media are all successful entrepreneurs, including Peter Thiel, who created PayPal and is also an early investor in Facebook. In other words, the investment had a lot of small advantages that added up and offered assurance that I wasn't making a mistake. The jury is still out, of course, but AceBucks is currently adding ten thousand to twenty thousand users a day and I never even worry about it.

The same is true for stock investments: Accumulate small advantages. Find people smarter than you and watch what they are doing. For instance, I know nothing about pork other than the fact that I can eat bacon three meals a day, ooze pig fat from all my pores, and still be happy in life. But when I hear that a director of pork producer Smithfield Foods (SFD) is buying millions of dollars' worth of stock on the open market, I take notice. When I also see that up to 20 percent of this year's pork output in China is off the market because it's riddled with disease and I see that Smithfield is the first company called to buy another 60 million pounds of pork, it further piques my interest. All of these things make me rest easier when recommending SFD as an investment, despite the fact that it's down 15 percent in the past three months. A bet on Smithfield stock is not a bet on 2008 or 2009 but a bet that a billion people who love to eat pork are going to use every means possible to get it, including calling American producers, as they become flush with enough cash to eat as much pork as they want.

The accumulation of small advantages can ease the amount of worry and thought you throw at a situation. Without these small advantages, the possibility of a big mistake greatly increases.

FOREVER FACEBOOK: WHY FACEBOOK IS WORTH $100 BILLION

I went on CNBC while I was in the middle of writing this book to talk about why I thought the social networking Web site Facebook was worth $100 billion.

Before my appearance, I was watching the hosts and they kept saying, "Stay tuned for a guy who thinks Facebook is worth $100 billion" and then they would cut to a video of Jeff Bezos laughing his head off. But the reality is, I don't think Facebook is like any normal Web site. Facebook is like a mini Internet. For a while I was jealous of Mark Zuckerberg, the company's young founder and CEO. Apparently he spurned an offer or two in the $600 million range, then the $1 billion range, and maybe even recently in the $2 billion range. I thought to myself at the time, "Man, that's the last time that kid is going to see those numbers." And I was right, but in the wrong direction: Recently Facebook sold a piece of itself to Microsoft at a $15 billion valuation.

After my bile subsided, I finally signed up for Facebook. It was incredible. It was like I'd been missing the best party of my life. Instantly all my VC buddies, writer friends, CEOs, and entrepreneurs were all messaging me through Facebook, "What took you so long?" I'm on there now about thirty times a day. It's a microcosm of the Internet that's neat and organized, and not only all of your friends, but all of your fantasy friends, are there. Bill Gates's page has fifty-seven friends on it, and he appears to be an active user. (He hasn't responded to my pleas for Facebook "friendship," but that's OK, I respect that.) Marc Cuban, Jim Cramer, Tom Glocer (CEO of Reuters), and about 30 million others are all regular users. A Facebook page cleanly sets up your interests, activities, and various Facebook applications that users collect. And if a Facebook page is like a mini personal Web site, the Facebook app universe has quickly become a microcosm of all the best Web applications out there.

I predict that:

- Every business, every business owner, and every advertiser is going to migrate to Facebook.
- Facebook applications are going to keep getting bigger, eventually providing real PayPal-style commerce and transactions.
- Advertisers are going to be able, for the first time ever, to do real broadcast microtargeting. DoubleClick has always attempted this by using cookies spread throughout its network, but Facebook has all the information in one place, with no real interpretation needed.
- Advertisers will kill each other to talk to the Facebook demographic. The teens are on here, they are using the apps, and the tightness of the

organization of content and information makes it a thousand times easier to target compared to MySpace. In addition, with the help of private companies like Lotame, which focuses on social-media marketing, the entire world of targeting within a site like Facebook is going to change rapidly over the next year, so rapidly that it will call into question the advertising models of just about every other Web site and media property.

In conclusion, once Facebook goes public at a $15–$20 billion valuation, be prepared to buy it. It's going to $100 billion, and then higher.

I know I mentioned a third mistake that I wanted to write about. But I think it's too personal.

2006 WORLDWIDE PORK CONSUMPTION

Region	Metric Tons (millions)	Per Capita (kg)
People's Republic of China	52.5	40.0
EU25	20.1	43.9
United States	8.7	29.0
Russian Federation	2.6	18.1
Japan	2.5	19.8
Others	12.2	n/a
Total	**98.9**	n/a

Source: *USDA Foreign Agricultural Service*, preliminary data for 2006.

20

Do You Want to Be a Forever Employee?
The Art of Reverse Exploitation

I t's not just the markets that are being changed by the trends that will occur over the next fifty years. The entire nature of a career will continue to change, as it has changed significantly over the past fifty years. It used to be the case that you'd work at a place, stay loyal, rise as high as you could, and receive a pension when you retired. That's no more. Now everyone has stories of the fifty-year-old who worked for two decades at a company until he was laid off without a day's notice. There's no loyalty anymore. But this isn't necessarily a bad thing.

Why is this section important in a book called *The Forever Portfolio*? Let's forget about the markets and stocks for a second. For one thing, as I write this, I'm a little bored with endless discussions of subprime and the supposed slowing of our economy. Whatever. The markets only get you somewhere between 5 and 20 percent a year. If you're a young person, that's meaningless. The only area where you can make consistent 100 percent per year returns, or more, is your career, whether you are an employee or an entrepreneur. No matter which you are, this where you need to focus right now. And to get the most out of your situation, you need to understand how to exploit your boss instead of the other way around.

In a capitalist economy, it's very clear that the Man needs to exploit the workers. When you run a company, the main challenges you have are to keep customers satisfied (and bring in new ones) and keep your workers exploited. For instance, in the nineties, I ran a company, Reset, which provided Web services to Fortune 100 companies like HBO, Disney, and Con Edison. I had two main responsibilities as CEO: selling our services to new customers, which required convincing clients they needed to spend $150,000 for a five-page Web site that very few people would visit. The second responsibility was making sure all of my employees were properly exploited. I mean this in a negative sense, but it doesn't have to be that way, for reasons I'll describe below.

The negative sense of exploitation is that I had to convince them to work eighteen hours a day, seven days a week, for pay that would allow me to make a maximum amount of money from their hourly efforts. Every single employer-employee situation on the planet works this way. You need people to work for less than what you're making. Not only that, you need them to expend maximum effort, and if they burn out along the way, then you need to squeeze every last drop of productivity out of them before they finally collapse and must be replaced. And don't fool yourself. Look around at all of your employees. At some point you will replace all of them, or at some point they will leave you in the dust when they realize it's time for them to move on. The age of four-decades-long exploitation culminating in a good-bye hug and a gold watch is long over.

But the beauty of capitalism now, as opposed to the factory-like economy that Marx was describing 140 years ago when he first outlined the map of exploitation, is that it's a two-way street. To succeed in life, the employee must exploit the employer as well, and I mean this in a positive way. At any given point, because of the liquidity of a global economy, because of the Internet, because of the vast array of opportunities in front of us, an employee must determine his or her worth on the market. This may entail constantly keeping your résumé out there (I recommend at least every one to two years getting your résumé in the hands of people who could make an offer); looking for opportunities on the side; continuing an education; building a documented description of your successes, so that no matter what happens to your job, you always have your accomplishments to point to; building connections between corporate departments so that no one supervisor can control your path through a company; interacting and socializing with the clients (external or internal) so that bridges can be crossed at critical tidal-wave moments; and a myriad other ways to move beyond the employer. This is not a negative. You are not end-running your employer—in fact, quite the contrary. Give your boss credit in every circumstance. Make him shine so bright that the light hides your own reverse exploitation. Everybody wins in a proper two-way exploitation, and capitalism thrives.

Here's my immediate five-step plan for employee-to-employer exploitation:

- **Give your boss credit for everything, and never talk poorly behind his or her back.** Never complain about being exploited. Exploit back. It doesn't matter if you are making $1 million a year as a top executive or $30,000 a year as a secretary. The higher up the job title is, the more the employee understands the need for reverse exploitation.
- **Make sure you have some contact, not through your boss, with every client he or she deals with.** Build your own reputation that you can point to when it comes time to leave.
- **Immediately send your résumé around.** You are not necessarily leaving, but if you haven't sent your résumé out in two years, then there is danger of becoming inbred. You must know what your value on the market is.
- **Always think about what skills you have that can last outside the corporate environment.** There is nothing wrong with

building a career and stability in the corporate environment, but always make sure you have skills that can survive outside of it. Be creative. Everyone can survive outside the corporate environment, even if it feels as though you can't. You can consult, start your own business, do anything. This is critical, and one way to get to this point is to make sure you improve your skills every single day. You must feel you've improved in some way each day.

- **Be productive.** There are eight hours in a typical workday, but the average employee works only a few of those hours. The rest of the time is spent on coffee breaks, Web surfing, lunch, random gossiping, useless meetings where everyone around a conference-room table is vying for attention. Try to spend at least four solid hours a day working.

If you follow these steps and continue to think, in a positive way, about how you can exploit your situation, then the effort you put into this will have much greater returns financially (and emotionally) than you can ever hope to have from investing in stocks. Exploitation is such a negative word, but if you aren't exploiting, then you're being exploited. That's guaranteed.

21

Internet Forever; or,
Five Mistakes I Made as a VC

bout ten years ago, I was in an elevator with Chubb Rock, the rapper. Our apartments were next to each other in the hotel we both lived in. And that's the last time I mention Chubb in this chapter, except to say that everything was possible in the nineties in New York. Economic growth was oozing out of the sidewalk and seeping into the cafés, onto the backs of napkins in diners, and into the offices that were springing out of nowhere in previously warehouse-ridden areas of the city. Everyone was raising money. But for what? For some of the stupidest ideas you've ever heard of. Portals for left-handed sports lovers, Geocities wannabes, calendar sites.

As an aside, I actually invested in a calendar site—Yourday.com. It was bought for break-even in restricted stock by the VoIP company deltathree when the stock was at $27. As I write this, it's at 15¢. As a further aside, there's the urban legend that the first online calendar was made by an NYU student in the mid-nineties and was bought by Yahoo! in 1996 for $10 million. I don't know if this is true or not.

Everything then was insane, and everyone was on an Indiana Jones–style hunt for the lost ark stuffed with money. I miss those days, because it's rare that the world we live in melds for a short time with the land of Oz, where wizards and witches grant immortality, love, or wisdom on those they favor. I feel I squandered that magic, or didn't quite know what to do with it back then, and only in brief moments I can summon it up again for a spell or two. Is it an age thing? I'm ten years older, after all, and just turned forty. Or are the 2000s different, with worry and fear dominating this decade instead of hope and greed? There's nothing wrong with greed. It creates railroads, grows beautiful tulips, and builds underwater cables to Europe and Web sites that sell millions of SKUs. But now every day I hear otherwise smart people tell me the consumer is dead, despite a bigger-than-expected increase in spending, a bigger-than-expected increase in incomes, and better GDP growth than expected. People are worried about "subslime" despite its being 1 percent of all mortgages. People are worried about inflation despite the Commerce Department price gauge being up only 1.9 percent from a year earlier. Others seem to be worried about deflation because housing is going down the drain and people will stop buying steel faucets and slate kitchens.

What happened to Y2K? That was the worry of the decade in the nineties—such an innocent one in retrospect. We were just children then, to have such a nonsense worry. But it was around that time that, with three other partners, I started a venture capital fund, 212 Ventures.

MISTAKE NO. 5: STARTING AT THE WRONG TIME

With any business venture, persistence is the key because factors such as the overall market are out of your control. That said, when

you have investors, partners, and employees, persistence becomes ex-
ponentially more difficult. We started 212 Ventures in March 2000
with $100 million in funding from Investcorp and another $15 million from UBS, CSFB, and Wachovia.

In March 2000, everybody knew it was a bubble. There wasn't a
single person out there who didn't think it was ridiculous when companies with no revenues were trading for $10 billion market caps
or more. But by March 2000, everything was so frothy that even
the biggest skeptic was starting to wonder if maybe, just maybe, it
could keep on going. As one of my partners at the time said to me,
"If only this thing can last just one more year. One more year, and
I'll be set."

Alas, it lasted about two more weeks, and then it was all over. Internet stocks began to slide, and on April 17, it was utter collapse
with the Nasdaq crash. The IPO window slid shut, but nobody knew
this for sure until September ("Wait for the fall," the investment
banks were saying all summer, "it will come back"), when people
realized we were in for the long haul. And then it just got worse and
worse. Fortunately, we had put relatively little money to work, but
there was just nothing at all to be excited about. From April 2000 on,
it was all damage control.

MISTAKE NO. 4: HOPING FOR SHORT-TERM GAINS

Our first investment was $5 million we put into an e-mail marketing
company started by a good friend and neighbor of mine, Lenny Barshak: bigfootinteractive.com. E-mail marketing, targeting, analytics,
promotions, and overall campaign management were increasingly
complicated for major corporations. The demographics were very
much on our side. E-mail and Internet users were still increasing in
double digits almost every month.

However, the company was spending money and building up

technical, support, and sales staff just when other companies were cutting back. Internet marketing was not as mainstream then as it's starting to be today, and everyone for a brief moment even thought the Internet was a big scam (including a partner of mine who quit the firm to become head of leverage finance at Bank of America).

So, in other words, the company needed to raise money. We introduced them to Donaldson, Lufkin & Jenrette (since acquired by Credit Suisse First Boston) and DLJ agreed to take it public. The S-1 was finished and they were all set to go when bam! The IPO door shut. There was no way to raise money from the public.

We put $5 million in the company, knowing that it was ready for an IPO (which meant something very different in March 2000 than it does today). We were all set for a quick tenfold return on our money as soon as the IPO happened. Then we would return some initial gains to our investors, knowing that life would be good for a long time afterward. When the company didn't go public, we weren't really prepared for the brutal reality of helping the company batten down the hatches and prepare for the long, hard grind.

Hundreds of employees were fired, costs were cut, and management teams were replaced. Lenny Barshak, who first brought me the deal, ended up leaving and starting an enormously profitable company in the online casino space. I first met Lenny, in fact, at the Mayfair Club, where I used to play poker every night until Mayor Rudolph Giuliani closed it down.

Eventually we merged the company with an e-mail marketing company funded by Flatiron Ventures, ratcheted down the investment (this was when I was no longer even with the VC firm), and it was just sold a few months ago for a solid triple on the investment. But it was this initial failure to meet our own expectations on the investment that was the beginning of the end for us.

MISTAKE NO. 3: FOCUSING TOO MUCH ON THE IPO MARKET

From the beginning I liked profitable companies. I liked Web services, online advertising, and some content plays. All three of these industries were largely profitable even in 2000, but they suffered collapses for different reasons by the time 2001 rolled around.

Web services—companies that helped other companies build Web sites—had been enormously profitable from 1996 to 2000. There were two primary customers: venture capital–funded companies and companies that had never heard of the Web but then suddenly realized they needed an online presence. The latter ranged from Fortune 10 firms like General Motors and American Express to tiny mom-and-pop shops that put up a one-page Web site.

To be in Web services was a money machine for several reasons. Large companies went through an evolution—first a single page, then a more comprehensive marketing brochure, then Web sites for every division, and finally full integration of the brand and customer communications with the Web presence. To build a relationship with a large company didn't mean just doing one Web site, but closer to a hundred Web sites during each phase of this evolution. And companies had no idea how much it cost to build a Web site, so Web service companies were charging up to $1,000 an hour, or more, to construct one. Then too, venture capitalists were pumping hundreds of millions of dollars into fledgling startups that were managed by inexperienced people who had no idea how to budget for technology or Web sites. Consequently, they got ripped off, and those hundreds of millions went, in part, into the pockets of Web service companies.

The entire industry died when the consumer Internet IPO bubble burst. VCs were no longer funding the latest portal for left-handed sports lovers (and yes, that business plan actually came across my desk). Now you can use sites like rentacoder.com or scriptlance.com to get your Web site or your entire e-commerce plan for almost nothing.

Online advertising suffered when the recession of 2001 forced companies to cut the experimental line item they had open for Internet advertising. People for a brief moment assumed that the Internet had just been a fad and that now it was all over. VC-funded companies stopped advertising, too. Moreover, because of the inherent accountability of Web traffic, people realized that banner advertising was not a good form if you wanted specific results (as opposed to brand advertising). The paradigm had not yet really shifted to reward pay-per-click advertising.

And content plays really suffered when the IPO market died. The traffic was not quite large enough to make content plays solidly profitable. Pay-per-click advertising had not yet been devised and infrastructure costs were too great. Now it's the reverse: The traffic is there, the business model (subscriptions and pay-per-click ads) is there, and infrastructure costs are nearly zero.

So, in fact, online advertising and content were the best business models to stick with. Instead, since the IPO market for those business models had shut down, my partners and I started exploring the fiber-optic services market—companies that provided consulting services to telecom companies to help them plan their fiber networks. Predictive Systems, in that space, had just gone public, and the stock was still soaring despite the shakeout in consumer Internet plays. Nevertheless, we had no real expertise in this area, and the small investments we made here came to nothing.

Our original premise, though—focusing on online advertising and content plays—is now proving to be the successful model of online business, Google being the ultimate example, but also MySpace, YouTube, Facebook, and others. We had the money, we had the initial premise, and, in a weird way, our timing was absolutely correct. If only we had ignored the whimsy of the IPO bankers and stayed the course.

MISTAKE NO. 2: NOT STICKING TO OUR GUNS

One of the big mistakes I made as a VC was not staying in the game. In 2001, our largest investor, Investcorp, essentially bought out our firm and gave us, the partners, the option to stick around. I decided to head for what I thought were greener pastures in the hedge-fund world.

I saw a short-term opportunity and decided to grab it. At the end of 2001 and throughout most of 2002, there were many companies that were breaking even or were profitable but had market caps less than the cash they had in the bank. I even wrote an article about ten such companies for *Street Insight* in December 2002.

Yet somewhere in my gut I knew that the Internet was only going to get larger, that it wasn't the fad everyone thought it was. Of course, my hunch proved to be correct. But while I was pursuing an investing game that lasted for just a brief period, the seeds of multibillion-dollar Internet opportunities were being sown right then in 2001. Google was developing its ad-auction model. MySpace was getting off the ground. Heck, hotornot.com was just launching, and soon the $1-million-per-month business with no employees— the dream of the Internet—would become a reality. These are the kind of opportunities that I hope I would have spotted and invested in had I stayed in the VC world.

IT'S HOT (THE INTERNET, THAT IS)

Hotornot.com actually makes for a fascinating case study that illustrates the incredible potential of the Internet. Two guys set this site up in a living room and promoted it by sending out e-mails to a bunch of their friends. Now, seven years later, hotornot.com has tallied more than 12 billion votes for and against men and women who were brave enough to submit photos for judgment. But how does a site like this make money, you ask? Simple: It's also a personals site.

And if you want to send a message to anyone who posts a photo on the site, you have to pay $5 a month. A hundred thousand people a month send in that $5. Yet it only costs about $500 a month to run a site like this.

OK, you may say, these guys were smart and got lucky, but there's no room for similar sites; it's too late. Well, I say look at plentyoffish .com, a free, easy-to-use dating site. You post a paragraph about yourself, upload a photo, and that's it. Done. You can then search for dates. This site's owner, Marcus Frind, makes about $400,000 a month and has no employees! He generates revenue from Google ad words.

So, I ask, is it too late? Are these little niches all taken up? I don't think so. Also, remember that there's still plenty of room for raw growth in the number of Internet users, according to Internet population statistics.

Only 51 percent of the United States is online right now, and only about 15 percent of people around the world are Internet users. And this doesn't really tell the full story. Most of those 51 percent in the United States who are online are still using dial-up modems; only about one-third of them have broadband. And even among broadband users, only a limited number are spending more than a few minutes a day online. The Internet is still in a nascent stage as a source of entertainment, commerce, and information.

MISTAKE NO. 1: BECOMING A VC IN THE FIRST PLACE

I wish I had tried out a few more of the ideas I had instead of sitting in my office waiting for ridiculous business plans to hit my desk. I was more reactive than proactive. Ideas are a dime a dozen, but I had the background and skill set to actually execute them. The costs of doing any one of them (like hotornot.com) were almost nothing, and I could've programmed up just about any idea myself. Sometimes it's better to do than to invest.

All of this is to say that the Internet is a hard trend to invest in.
The barrier of entry is extremely low. Even with a brand and user
base as strong as the ones Yahoo! had, a Google can come right in
and scoop up all of the market share. Or consider Newscorp's
MySpace; it's the leading social network right now, but it's quickly
being eclipsed by Facebook.

Anyway, here's the direction I would go when constructing an Internet forever portfolio, and it's going to be the obvious: Buy Google
(GOOG).

**GOOGLE, INC. CLASS A COMMON STOCK
as of Apr. 24, 2008**

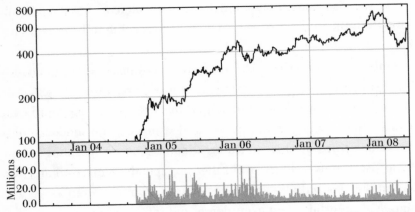

Copyright 2008 Yahoo! Inc.   http://finance.yahoo.com

Google dominates search, video, and online advertising, and eventually it will dominate offline advertising. I don't care what the P/E
ratio is. I don't even care what the actual percentages are that it
dominates in each area. Every year for the next fifty years, it will
probably go up in each category. It's worth a long-term bet even if
there's short-term volatility year by year.

Here's another suggestion for an Internet forever portfolio, but it's
also related to another trend that I mentioned briefly in chapter 18—
the nonstop decrease in auto safety.

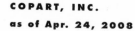

COPART, INC.

as of Apr. 24, 2008

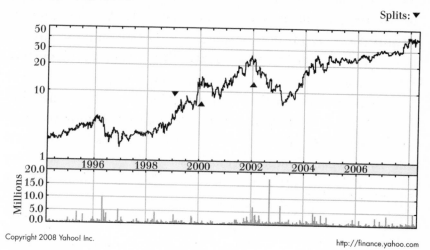

http://finance.yahoo.com

Let's say you're in an auto accident and you're entitled to money from the insurance company. The adjuster looks at the car and, through a variety of methods, determines that it's totaled, meaning it will cost the insurer more to repair the car than to just pay out the money to buy a new one. So what does the company do with your car now? They're not really equipped to store tens of thousands of wrecked cars and deal with taking them apart and selling off the pieces as scrap.

Copart (CPRT) has a lock on this business. It handles storage, transfer of ownership, and every aspect of the transaction that insurance companies just don't want to deal with. For the most part, Copart sells the wrecked cars in online auctions to people who are willing to repair and resell them, or pull them apart when the salvageable parts are worth more than what's left of the cars.

The business is also economy independent. Copart's revenue from 2000 to 2004 (through recession and boom) increased steadily: In 2000, the company reported $190 million; in 2001, $253 million; in 2002, $316 million; in 2003, $347 million; and in 2004, $400 million. With more than 6 million auto accidents in the world each year, it's guaranteed that the economy will have nothing to do with the success or failure of this company.

I also like the fact that solid, value-oriented funds—Blue Harbour Group, Royce & Associates, and the activist fund Jana Partners—are all major shareholders; they all tend to be long-term holders. This is also one of the few Internet businesses that Google probably will have no interest in competing with. Let's say you believe that the rise in health-care problems will benefit companies like WebMD. Once Google puts significant resources behind a "Google Health," though, all bets are off in that space. Google simply dominates the world, so let's keep that in mind for our forever portfolios.

DOMAIN NAMES

Speaking of world domination, I'm jealous. Not of the usual suspects. I am fine with all the thirtysomething hedge-fund managers making $20 million bonuses. I have dealt with the fact that there are managing directors at the big investment banks who earn $10 million a year. That's fine. I don't want to work at an investment bank. Lloyd Blankfein at Goldman Sachs did not respond to my e-mails six years ago anyway.

No, I'm jealous of the people who registered names like sex.com, vodka.com, and business.com. Sex.com sold for $12 million in 2005 to a private equity group. Vodka.com sold for $2 million, business .com for $7.5 million in 1999. The list goes on. Even the misspelled mortage.com garnered $242,000. These were smart people who registered these names.

We all knew, back in the early 1990s, that the Internet was going to be big. But few had the business sense to make a land grab on domain names. It was even free to register then.

Cover this paper for a second and try to guess the first .com registered. Your hunch might be ibm.com or microsoft.com, but that is not the case. The first was symbolics.com. Symbolics, Inc. was a spin-off of MIT that made Lisp machines. Do you use a Lisp machine?

It's natural that the domain-name business would intersect with the hedge-fund world. I called Jeff Burkey, who runs hedgefund domain.net. He sells domains for hedge funds. Say you were an amateur pilot paying your dues at Goldman Sachs and now you're ready to start your own hedge fund. You had your heart set on Aviator Capital but aviatorcapital.com is already taken. No sweat—Burkey owns it. And he has it for sale for $10,000.

That is nothing if you're launching a $700 million hedge fund. He has great names for sale, including maximacapital.com and lucentcapital.com, each for $10,000. "The theory is similar to a deep-out-of-the-money option strategy," he said. "Since I buy all the domains directly from the registrar, my cost is very low, less than $10 per year," Burkey said. "I buy most knowing full well they will expire worthless. I only need a few to hit for a solid ROI."

The idea was born when he tried to register a domain name, terrapincapital.com. "It was taken, so I registered two derivatives, diamondbackcapital.com and testudocapital.com." A few months later Chad Loweth and others started a $500 million fund and happened to name it Diamondback Capital. "So I learnt a little HTML, and hedgefunddomain.net went live. It's been a lot of fun."

When I spoke to Burkey, vodka.com had just been sold for $2 million and he'd been trying to register whiskey.com, sherry.com, and others. Of course, they were all taken. It turned out that Bob Chapman, a hedge-fund manager and shareholder activist, owned sherry.com. I rang Bob and asked when he started buying domain names.

"In March 1996, it was obvious to me that .com versus .net, et cetera, was beachfront real estate available for lease at $35 a year. A true no-brainer," he said. Had he received offers for any of the domain names he owns? "Yes," he said, "but they were not bought with an intent to sell for a profit, instead to use them. Several telco service operators have offered me over $3 million for calls.com—to compete against Skype—but I am holding out for a much higher price. Given that all calls are going to be made over the Internet in the next ten years, calls.com is the hotels.com of that space."

Several public companies in the domain-name business are worthy of inclusion in a forever portfolio. First, there is Marchex (MCHX), started by Russ Horowitz, former Go2Net founder and chief executive. The company owns more than 200,000 names, including domains for every zip code.

Communicate.com (CMNN.ob, which trades over the counter) is a small public company that is sitting on quite a few domain names, including importers.com, perfume.com, body.com, and cricket.com. The company has been generating revenue by selling domain names but also, more recently, by setting up e-commerce sites on some of these domains and making decent money from retail.

Tucows (TCX), another Amex-listed company, helps connect buyers and sellers of domain names and takes fees in the middle. Tucows is currently the fourth largest domain-name registrar.

The private company GoDaddy is in first place. GoDaddy is a veritable cash machine but pulled its S-1 filing because it didn't like how GAAP (Generally Accepted Accounting Principles) forced it to defer, sometimes for years, cash revenues the company already had in the bank. "There's no need for us to go public," Bob Parsons, chief executive, said at the time.

However, the granddaddy of the domain-name business is VeriSign (VRSN), which is the provider of all the .com and .net domain names. All of the registrars are simply reselling domain names they acquire through VeriSign.

22

Generating Ideas That Last Forever; or, Investing in Your Business/Ideas

I'm coming to grips with the fact that I'm a somewhat unpleasant person. I don't really like vacations, for instance. And I hate holidays. They all just seem like stressful work to me. I can't stand beaches, and having to drive hours for a meal with family members isn't such a hot idea. I also don't like animals at all. I took my kids to Petco, and I found the entire experience thoroughly disgusting. There were rats and ferrets in cages and the place smelled terrible. My kids were begging me to get *Rats* magazine with "150 full color pictures" for them. Who would even write for such a magazine?

I love my kids, but when it comes to helping them get up in the morning and feeding them, I'll pass. That's just hard work, and I like to avoid that. What I like to do in the morning is get up really early, before anyone else in my house gets up—even on Saturdays and Sundays—and take my waiter's pad to the local café.

I bought about five hundred waiter's pads for 25¢ each online from a restaurant-supply site. Waiter's pads are excellent for listing things, and the pad fits right in your pocket. So each morning, I sit down at the café, get a coffee, read a newspaper or two, and then list ideas. I've been doing this every day without fail since mid-2002. I list ideas for anything: investments, trading systems, businesses, books, articles—and ideas for other people, which provides a very effective way to contact them, particularly if you don't know them. I don't hold back. It's critical to constantly exercise the "idea muscle," or it quickly atrophies. After that point, it can only be built back up with months, maybe years, of therapy.

I started doing this in 2002 because I wanted to trade for a hedge fund and I also wanted to write. But when I wrote to hedge funds or publications I got back zero responses despite my résumé as a fund manager, venture capitalist, and entrepreneur. So instead of asking for something for myself, I gave something instead.

I wrote twenty e-mails to fund managers and publications, giving ideas for trading systems and article ideas. I received two responses. One was from Jim Cramer asking me if I wanted to write for TheStreet.com. I had approached him asking to write about something I called preferred arbitrage, an idea based on the fact that there were many preferred stocks at that time yielding more than 15 percent that were just as volatile as the underlying common stock. You could go long Duke Energy preferred, for instance, and short Duke and lock in the 15 percent yield. I ended up writing about this for TheStreet.com, which ultimately led to a weekly column for the *Financial Times.*

I also wrote a fund manager based in Connecticut with a system for trading futures when things were particularly volatile. He ended up allocating some money for me, and the trading system did very well until eventually I started a fund of funds.

So let's brainstorm on businesses we can start. The key here is to not worry about whether you are having good ideas or bad ideas. Just have many ideas.

Don't be afraid to come up with bad ideas. For instance, I set up a dating site for smokers only about a year ago. Bad idea: SmokeLove

.com was almost immediately hijacked by spammers, and I decided to give up. Here's another bad idea I had—a really horrible idea. I wanted to emulate hotornot.com (good idea), so I made smartorstupid.com (bad idea). The concept was, everyone who signs up takes an IQ test, then viewers would judge members "smart" or "stupid," depending on whether they look intelligent or not. Further, if viewers liked what they saw, they could enter the online dating part of the site. A few hundred people signed up fairly quickly, but even my eight-year-old daughter said to me, when I showed her the site, "But Daddy, isn't this kind of mean?" And she was right. It was mean! There was a minuscule chance for the site to be successful, but I had to try. It's cheap to try any idea you want. Use a site like scriptlance.com, find yourself a good developer from Siberia who will program in C++ and Java for $3 an hour from his igloo, and build whatever business you want.

Then I set up Stockpickr.com, which is sort of a MySpace for finance (see chapter 15). Members enter their portfolios, I match the portfolio with some of the other ninety thousand portfolios in the site (including eight hundred hedge-fund or superinvestor portfolios like those of Warren Buffett and George Soros), and then recommendations are generated. There's also the usual stuff: forums, blogs, an "Answers" section like Yahoo! Answers, and about twenty other features.

This site (unlike the dating site for smokers) came out of real love and passion (whereas my last cigarette was at age thirteen). It's been a blast! I can't talk numbers (we were acquired recently by TheStreet.com, a public company), but it's been amazing to see a growing community that really makes use of something I've built. I love it. Every new feature or module in the site has been something we've used at some point over the past seven or eight years to generate ideas for our trading and investing. We threw everything in there, and continue to add to it.

So what's still out there, and how can you profit from it? Here's another idea: I think there's huge opportunity over the next fifty years to start a natural-search marketing company. There are very few public companies focused on this (Think Partnership (THK) is the only pure play), and the potential is immense. People are giving Google billions of dollars so that links to their products and companies appear to the right of a search on google.com. But companies are loath to spend money to simply improve their natural-search results (i.e., where they come up in the unpaid search results). Yet almost every Web site I visit can easily make use of nine or ten techniques to improve their results, things I can spot just by looking at the site. How much would companies pay to improve those results? A lot, and I know this because it's a better use of money than the billions corporate America pays Google just to appear on the right-hand side of the page, which almost everyone ignores.

OK, here's another great business idea to be on the lookout for: autofingerprinting all videos by the ratio of red to blue to green in each clip. Right now fingerprinting is being done at the production level by adding in some extra pixels that are unnoticeable when video is cut. But why not do it postproduction and constantly search video sites for unlicensed uses of the fingerprint?

Or what about a portal for class-action lawsuits? For instance, if you ate McDonald's French fries a few years ago, you might have a case, as vegetarians were not informed that beef fat was used in the fries. There are thousands of cases like this, and almost everyone in the country—from smokers to stock investors—is entitled to money in dozens of class-action lawsuits. A portal would connect people with the lawsuits that potentially could include them. Why is this valuable? A law firm can make more than $1,000 for each client who is directed toward it. How much will that firm pay for the client? How about a hundred thousand of those clients?

More ideas: I like business models such as the one that Red Hat applied to the Linux operating system. This company decided to make Linux enterprise-friendly, despite it being a free operating system made by hundreds of contributing programmers, and they gave the package away for nothing—just bundled with a service contract that includes maintenance and upgrades. Brilliant! In the past twelve months, Red Hat had almost $200 million in cash flows. So here's the new twist. Most startup Internet companies, including Stockpickr.com, use the free database software MySQL and the free programming language PHP to quickly prototype and develop their applications. Believe me, using PHP/MySQL, you can build a complete duplicate to YouTube in under three weeks (I did it with funnyorflat.com). But PHP/MySQL are far from enterprise-friendly, for various reasons. Suffice it to say nobody will build industrial-strength applications that way, so let's do with PHP/MySQL what Red Hat did for Linux: make it enterprise-friendly and bundle in maintenance. If you make just a small dent in Oracle and SAP (it's not that hard to do), then it's a multibillion-dollar company.

Here's another one: Nobody has yet created a national chain of falafel fast-food outlets in the United States. In Manhattan, there are lines down the block for good falafel. But it usually hails from small, family-run places, very crowded and uncomfortable, with cheap furniture and smoke from the grill in your eyes. So let's give falafel the McDonald's treatment: sterilize the shops, make each outlet the same, focus on the vegetable accompaniments and the health aspects, streamline the process, give everyone uniforms, and play top 20 music. Then take it national. You could have the Jamba Juice of falafel.

23

Bloody Marys, Dividends, and the San Francisco Earthquake

I once sat next to an economics consultant on a plane who, over a drink, told me the secret to all market returns. First of all, what's an economics consultant? And second, why is it that people drink tomato juice on planes but never anywhere else? When I'm flying, it's often the case that everyone around me is drinking either a Bloody Mary or straight tomato juice. But I've never seen people drink these anywhere else. If anyone has an answer, please e-mail me at james@formulacapital.com.

In any case, this consultant—let's call him DM—who's also a well-known blogger and financial writer, was going to visit one of his clients. His clients are mostly top-tier banks, hedge funds, and megafamily offices in the billion-dollar-plus category. They pay him anywhere from $5,000 to $20,000 per month to have him on call. When he isn't visiting one of his clients or making one of his regular appearances on CNBC, he's basically sitting on the steps of the Federal Reserve waiting for various Fed governors to come out and whisper secrets in his ear, which they often do. He also eats steak for breakfast, lunch, and dinner (no carbs) and lifts weights constantly. When his clients call him, they want guidance on where bonds are going, where commodities are going, what his take on currencies is, and of course, what he thinks the stock market will do. At one point in his career he managed about $100 billion for a large bank. So his guess is often pretty good, and, most important, he loves his job.

"There's one thing the markets care about," he told me while sipping his tomato juice. "Inflation."

"But inflation's been at 1 to 4 percent forever," was my reply. "What more can the markets want? Doesn't the market care about things like subprime or tech?"

"Sure," he said, "but all of that's a by-product. Everything falls apart if we have inflation. Now note, it doesn't matter what inflation is right now. It only matters what inflation is in the future. The market couldn't care less what inflation is right now. But it always wants to know that the Fed has a grip on it and there's basically zero chance that it could get out of control. Sometimes the Fed has to talk down the economy so it can lower interest rates. If people think the economy is strong and the Fed is lowering interest rates, then the worry will be that inflation will get out of control and we'll get a scenario where interest rates are going lower and the market is crashing."

"Does Bernanke know what he's doing?" I asked.

"Bernanke was 'Helicopter Ben' when the market was worried about deflation in 2002," DM replied. "He was ready to drop dollar bills on the market in order to stir things up. But let's not forget the guy was an expert on the Great Depression. That's what he's written all his academic papers on. He knows what to do. But, of course, he's not dominating the board like Greenspan did. So let's see what he can do."

In this entire book, this is the only place I've written more than a couple of words about the Federal Reserve. And the conclusion I'm going to derive from this discussion with DM has nothing to do with the Fed, the overall market, interest rates, or inflation. In fact, I really don't like thinking about all that stuff. The Fed is the subject of endless debates on TV. But what does it all mean? People think the market will go up once the Fed starts cutting rates. But what happened in 2001–02 when the Fed was massively cutting every chance it could get? The market went straight down. And when the Fed was raising rates in 1999, what happened? The market went straight up. So gaming the Fed doesn't really have much predictive value in the markets.

Why bring all this up now? Well, the one insight DM had was that people love consistency. They crave it. They go insane without it. If your spouse comes home from work every night at 7:00 p.m. and one evening he or she comes home at 7:30 p.m. because of a missed train, then you start to worry. What led to the inconsistency, could it happen again, could it be a symptom of a problem much deeper, something that could force your entire life to be rethought and then spun out of control? Could things get really bad really fast just because your spouse is home a half-hour late? Well, maybe.

So consistency is important. And it's critically important because consistency breeds more consistency. If the sun has always risen, then chances are it will rise tomorrow. A forever portfolio must allow us to rest easy at night, knowing that our children and grandchildren will be protected by the fruits of these investments fifty years out. If we don't bet on consistency, then all hope is lost.

Fortunately, we have some friends to help us with this. The S&P 500 has been kind enough to provide us with the Dividend Aristocrats, which is a list of all S&P 500 companies that have increased their dividends every year for twenty-five straight years or more. Companies increase their dividends for a variety of reasons, some good and some bad:

- They want to artificially, and temporarily, increase their stock price by having a nice press release announcing the dividend increase.
- They want to appease an activist shareholder who is demanding they return cash to shareholders.
- They want to be attractive to a type of investor who is looking for yield, so they feel compelled to get their dividend above a certain level.

However, a company can only increase its dividend for twenty-five years in a row if its profits are rising. This demonstrates that the company is being run by effective management. A dividend is very difficult to reduce without drastically affecting a company's stock price (because investors will then lose that consistency), so a company seldom increases its dividend without having a high degree of confidence that profits over the coming years will be more than sufficient to pay that dividend. In fact, academic research has shown that an increase in dividends is predictive of future earnings increases.

Jeremy Siegel, a professor at Wharton who wrote the classic book *Stocks for the Long Run*, has some fascinating data about dividends in his recent book *The Future for Investors*. For one thing, Siegel demonstrates that since 1871, the inflation-adjusted returns of the stock market have come almost entirely from dividends. Specifically, if you had always reinvested dividends back into the market, 97 percent of your gains would've come from dividends and only 3 percent from capital gains (i.e., from stock appreciation). He also notes that the twenty best-performing stocks of the original S&P 500 formed in 1957 are all dividend-paying stocks. Here is a sampling of these stocks, courtesy of the Motley Fool:

Company	Dividend Yield	Annual Return	$1,000 Invested
Philip Morris (MO)	4.07%	19.75%	$4,626,402
Tootsie Roll (TR)	2.44%	16.11%	$1,090,955
Merck (MRK)	2.37%	15.90%	$1,003,410
Crane (CR)	3.62%	15.14%	$736,796
Fortune Brands (FO)	5.31%	14.55%	$580,025
Procter & Gamble (PG)	2.75%	14.26%	$513,752
Royal Dutch Petroleum (RD)	5.24%	13.64%	$398,837
S&P 500	3.27%	10.85%	$124,486

Source: Jeremy Siegel, *The Future for Investors*

It's interesting that, in his article "Ben Bernanke's Favorite Stock," written for Yahoo! Finance in November 2005, Siegel points out that when Bernanke was selected as Fed chairman (and had to disclose his holdings), he only owned one stock: Altria Group (MO), formerly Philip Morris. Bernanke, too, clearly likes dividend-increasing consistency.

In that article, Siegel points out a few more things about Philip Morris. For example, "Since 1992, the average dividend yield of Philip Morris has been 5.2 percent, versus only 1.9 percent for the S&P 500 Index. . . . Philip Morris also disproves the oft-heard Wall Street assertion that fast-growing firms should not pay dividends. MO managed to grow (in fact, the company delivered some of the highest earnings-growth rates I've found in my studies) and still pay a hefty dividend check to shareholders." It's no surprise that Philip Morris is in the Dividend Aristocrats club that the S&P has compiled, having increased its dividend for more than twenty-five straight years.

ALTRIA GROUP
as of Feb. 15, 2008

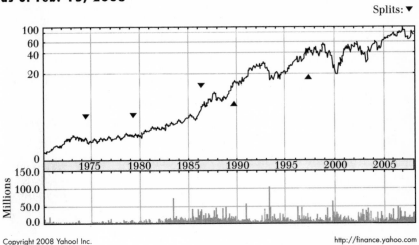

S&P has compiled some data on how these stocks have performed. Over the past seven years, starting in 2001, with data coming from bull markets, bear markets, and volatile markets, the S&P Dividend Aristocrats index has returned 8 percent per year versus 3 percent per year for the S&P 500, handily outperforming its non-dividend-paying colleagues. Most of this outperformance stems from the way the index held up in 2002. In a bear market, dividend-paying stocks will perform OK compared to hyped stocks that tend to crash and burn faster than the dividend-paying stocks or the "boring" stocks we discussed earlier.

S&P also put out a paper detailing its approach in developing the Dividend Aristocrats index. It notes this interesting statistic, which is related to the aging Baby Boomers (see chapter 12): "In 2004, dividend income comprised 4.6% of per capita personal income in the U.S., compared to 2.7% 20 years prior. In terms of year 2000 dollars, total personal dividend income increased from $134 billion to $407 billion. During the same period, the other source of income from capital markets, interest, saw its share in personal income shrink from 15.7% to 9.8%."

But the kicker is this: "As equity ownership becomes even more ubiquitous, and a growing number of retiring Americans seek income-generating assets, the importance of personal dividend income shall increase." In other words, as Baby Boomers begin retiring, which they are about to do in droves, the reliance on the dividends paid from stocks is going to increase. And how will people know which stocks are most likely to continue paying (or increase) dividends? They'll buy the stocks that have consistently increased.

The paper uses various statistical measures to compare the Dividend Aristocrats with other indices, particularly the S&P 500 index. It then concludes:

1. The Aristocrats have outperformed the S&P 500 over the past five, ten, and fifteen years.
2. The Aristocrats have had lower risk than the S&P 500 over all time periods considered.

So let's take a look at some of the Aristocrats. We've already seen MO.

Bank of America (BAC) is one of Warren Buffett's favorite stocks. As I write this, he recently doubled down, so that now he owns 20 million shares of the bank's $1.5 trillion in assets. Furthermore, Bank of America has a rich history, more dramatic than having simply raised its dividend for twenty-five straight years.

The bank was started in 1904 by Amadeo Giannini and was originally called the Bank of Italy. When the great earthquake shook San Francisco to the ground in 1906, Giannini saved all the money from the burning bank and escaped with his life. Two days later, his was the first bank to reopen, calming all the anxious customers who were worried about losing their life savings.

That consistency has done well for shareholders over time. The chart (see page 219) does not fully reflect the gains shareholders would've received if they had reinvested the dividend, which now sits at 7 percent.

BANK OF AMERICA CORP.

as of Feb. 15, 2008

Splits: ▼

http://finance.yahoo.com

Two other Buffett favorites are members of the Dividend Aristocrats: U.S. Bancorp (USB) and Johnson & Johnson (JNJ). See chapter 3
regarding the latter.

Another solid, steady earner is Johnson Controls (JCI). This company makes auto-body parts and interiors as well as car batteries. It
also helps maintain buildings.

JOHNSON CONTROLS

as of Feb. 15, 2008

Splits: ▼

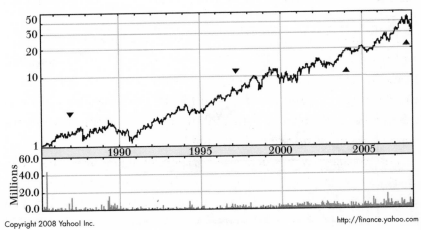

http://finance.yahoo.com

W. W. Grainger (GWW), also in the building supplies and main-tenance business, has raised its dividend for more than twenty-five straight years.

GRAINGER (WW)
as of Feb. 25, 2008

Copyright 2008 Yahoo! Inc.   http://finance.yahoo.com

Pfizer (PFE), maker of both Zoloft and Viagra, among other drugs, is in the club. And, at the time of this writing, PFE yields 5.7 percent.

PFIZER, INC.
as of Feb. 15, 2008

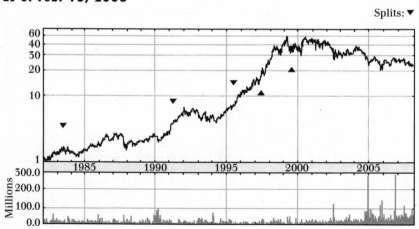

Copyright 2008 Yahoo! Inc.   http://finance.yahoo.com

Another pharmaceutical company, Eli Lilly (LLY), is also a Dividend Aristocrat.

LILLY (ELI) & CO.
as of Feb. 15, 2008

Splits: ▼

Copyright 2008 Yahoo! Inc.   http://fianace.yahoo.com

A LOW-RISK ALTERNATIVE TO THE ARISTOCRATS

I want to mention one more method for accumulating dividends in a relatively risk-free manner that is good for long-term/forever-style investing.

A few years ago I wrote an article describing how I was allocating my mom's portfolio. She had some money after my father passed away and she had two conditions for how she wanted it allocated. She wanted approximately 8 percent yield for income and she wanted it to be as risk free as possible.

Around the same time I had a discussion with a hedge fund manager who had extra cash that he was allocating for his personal account. He told me he was going to put it (about $100 million) in municipal bonds. I suggested to him the same idea I used to allocate my mom's portfolio.

His response, "That's great! I don't know why I didn't think of that."

The idea is to put your money in closed end funds that specialize in high yielding bonds but only pick the closed end funds that are trading at significant discounts to their net asset value. Closed end funds (as opposed to mutual funds) trade all day long on the various stock exchanges and, depending on investor sentiment, often trade below the value of all their holdings added together.

Example: As I write this, the Global Income Fund (symbol: GIFD) is trading at a 15 percent discount to its net asset value and has a yield of 6.5 percent. This is the largest discount to its net asset value since 2000 and it has historically been able to close its discount over time. Are its assets risky? Its largest holdings are government bonds from Austria and Sweden and no position greater than 4 percent. So it's not so risky. Potentially one can get a 15 percent boost when it closes its discount to its net asset value and, while you wait, you can collect the 6.5 percent dividend. There are also opportunities using the Dividend Achievers to maximize returns with similar risk.

Finally, I'd like to quote again from the S&P document "Introducing the S&P 500 Dividend Aristocrats Index," which can be found on the following page, 223, through page 225.

S&P 500 DIVIDEND ARISTOCRATS
As of January 16, 2008

Company	Ticker
3M Company	MMM
Abbott Laboratories	ABT
Aflac, Inc.	AFL
Air Products and Chemicals	APD
Anheuser-Busch	BUD
Archer Daniels Midland	ADM
Automatic Data Processing, Inc.	ADP
Avery Dennison Corp.	AVY
Bank of America Corp.	BAC
C. R. Bard, Inc.	BCR
BB&T Corporation	BBT
Becton, Dickinson and Co.	BDX
CenturyTel	CTL
Chubb Corp.	CB
Cincinnati Financial Corp.	CINF
Clorox Co.	CLX
Coca-Cola Co.	KO
Comerica Inc.	CMA
Consolidated Edison	ED
Dover Corp.	DOV
Emerson Electric Co.	EMR
ExxonMobil Corp.	XOM
Family Dollar Stores	FDO
Fifth Third Bancorp	FITB
Gannett Co., Inc.	GCI
General Electric	GE

Company	Ticker
W. W. Grainger, Inc.	GWW
Integrys Energy Group, Inc.	TEG
Johnson & Johnson	JNJ
Johnson Controls, Inc.	JCI
KeyCorp	KEY
Kimberly-Clark	KMB
Leggett & Platt, Inc.	LEG
Eli Lilly & Co.	LLY
Lowe's Companies	LOW
M&T Bank Corp.	MTB
McDonald's Corp.	MCD
McGraw-Hill	MHP
Nucor Corp.	NUE
PepsiCo, Inc.	PEP
Pfizer, Inc.	PFE
Pitney Bowes	PBI
PPG Industries	PPG
Procter & Gamble	PG
Progressive Corp.	PGR
Questar Corp.	STR
Regions Financial Corp.	RF
Rohm and Haas	ROH
Sherwin-Williams	SHW
Sigma-Aldrich	SIAL
Stanley Works	SWK
State Street Corp.	STT

Company	Ticker
SuperValu, Inc.	SVU
Target Corp.	TGT
U.S. Bancorp	USB
VF Corp.	VFC
Walgreens	WAG
Wal-Mart Stores	WMT
William Wrigley Jr. Co.	WWY

24

Can You Live and Invest Forever?

I know this sounds crazy, but forty years old is *old.* I turned forty in January 2008, and I'm feeling it. The other day I was reading the book *Summer of '49* by David Halberstam, about the Yankees season in 1949. In it, he comments how the Yankees team was going to have problems because of its aging players. For instance, "DiMaggio's body was breaking down." You would think he was ninety years old from that description. DiMaggio was thirty-four at the time. So I put that book down and opened up *Chess Life* magazine. It always conjures up memories of hanging out at the Manhattan Chess Club as a kid, all the old men stroking their beards, pondering moves for hours. I turned to an article about the top twenty chess players in the world, and the author mentioned there are only two "old-timers" on the list: Viswanathan Anand, age thirty-eight, and Boris Gelfand, age thirty-seven. Great. I guess I'm too old for even no-impact sports, too.

Then a friend called me. He was applying for a prop trading position at a tier-one bank. "I barely made the cutoff," he said. "I'm twenty-nine and they aren't hiring anyone over thirty." In a world where productive life spans are getting longer, thanks to medical technology, the pressure to succeed is hitting ambitious people at ever younger ages. At what point does my résumé transform itself from "string of successes" to "dilettante"? To be honest, it's starting to unnerve me.

So I did what I usually do when I'm down about something. I called up a friend to cheer me up. This time I decided to call John Pappajohn. I called him for three very important reasons. One, he's the most successful investor I know, having returned 60 percent per year since he started his investing career (and having given most of it away to charity along the way). Two, at seventy-nine, he's very insightful, and almost double my age. And three, he began his career at the age of forty-one, in 1969. Since then he's started more than fifty health-care companies that eventually made their way into the public marketplace, including Caremark.

"You're calling for what reason? What!?" he asked and then laughed. "Listen, it only gets better," he said, "I have seven financings going on, a company I'm involved in that might go public soon, and we just did a reverse merger with another company. Things are better than ever."

"But, John," I asked him, "when you started your first venture deal at the age of forty-one, were you a little scared?"

"Oh sure, you're always apprehensive. That's normal. And heck, this was 1969; hardly anybody was in venture capital back then, and I decided to go into it. I called up another investor, Warren Buffett, and he told me, 'John, you're making a mistake.' He told me he was getting out of the business and going into operating a company. And you know what, James, he was right. Interest rates went to 16 percent, the economy went into a horrible recession, the venture business was dead. I was doing little M & A deals to make a living, but that's it."

My friend told me great stories: "I started my venture business with a hundred thousand dollars. That's all. My wife and I drove around in old cars, we lived within our means, but I always kept a

PMA—positive mental attitude. I always held on to that. And then I started a company, Kay Laboratories, which eventually merged into Baxter. I started Caremark, which grew much bigger. Then I started Medical Imaging Laboratories. Altogether I've been involved in fifty companies that eventually got bought or went public, all in the medical space.

"And I'll tell you why it gets better. Everyone always calls me now when they have a deal. I've been around long enough so I get to know everybody. Keep your nose clean, build good relationships over the years, and people will keep showing you good deals. In one deal that I did ten or fifteen years ago, for Quantum Health Resources, the founder, Doug Stickney, offered me the opportunity to invest two hundred thousand dollars because he liked the way I had dealt with his father on an earlier deal. Well, that two hundred thousand dollars was worth sixty million dollars six years later. And you know what, James, Doug just called me two weeks ago with another deal and wanted to know if I would be interested. Sure I would be!"

Pappajohn has definitely been keeping busy. He's involved with several public companies, including a SPAC (Special Purpose Acquisition Company) called Healthcare Acquisition Corp. (HAQ); American Caresource Holdings (XSI); Allion Healthcare (ALLI), which offers disease-management services for HIV patients, has $20 million cash in the bank, and trades for 18 times cash flow; and the elder care–management company CareGuide (CGDE). Additionally, he's working on a reverse merger with a company that provides health care to county jails.

Also, one thing that I think keeps Pappajohn exuberant and excited about coming to work every day is that he gives an enormous amount to charity, such as the John and Mary Pappajohn Clinical Cancer Center, affiliated with the University of Iowa. "Giving money away is a prerequisite to making more money. When you get older," he told me, "you have to keep thinking of new ways to create value. That's important."

25

The Forever Student

Things are simpler than they appear. I'll give you an example. Let's say you want to beat everyone in your family at Scrabble. You have two choices. You can read every book you can find, build an enormous vocabulary, look up the definitions of words you don't know (that will help you remember them better), and use your advanced knowledge, painstakingly constructed over years, to defeat all opponents.

Or you can remember the following five words: *xi, xu, za, qi,* and *qat. Ka* and *ki* are not so bad either. And every now and then *aa, ae,* and *ai* can prove incredibly useful. These are all legal words in the last edition of the official Scrabble dictionary. What do they mean? I have no idea. You don't need to know. Somehow, though, *za* is slang for *pizza.* I've never heard that before, nor will I ever use the word *za* in place of *pizza.* Apparently it's used on the West Coast, but I've never heard anyone from there use the word *za.* Apparently, people from Trenton, N.J., use the phrase *tomato pies* instead of *pizza,* but I grew up twenty minutes from there and never heard anyone use that term, either. Some things are mysteries.

Once you are OK with the fact that *xu* is a legal word, then that means you can essentially slap that X down on a triple-letter score with much greater ease than any of your opponents really thought possible. While they are all stuck with their Qs and Zs, you're racking up fifty-point two-letter words and winning the game. The same economy of effort works for poker (see chapter 13).

I taught my eight-year-old daughter how to play poker the other day. Since I'm dead-set against the idea of her going to college, I figure she might as well get some skills as a gambler. Every time she's about to lie to me in poker, she looks to the left. Once I told her she did that, she sometimes looked to the left on purpose to make me think she was lying when she was actually telling the truth. When you tell your opponent something, and then they try to use that information against you, but you know in advance they will do so, that's called controlling your opponent. She became a fool twice over and had no chance while I took all her money. But it was a learning experience for her.

DON'T GO TO COLLEGE

I said I have no intention of sending my kids to college. And this is the crux of the matter, I feel, for young people who want to be successful over the next fifty-year period. I find the thought of college these days abhorrent, particularly for kids aged eighteen to twenty. Kids have a lot of energy at that point, and to deaden it with a forced, unsupervised diversity of random topics taught by mostly mediocre professors is a waste of it. I can't remember anything good coming from my freshman year other than that I started a business with a few of my classmates that inspired me for other businesses later on. We set up a business called CollegeCard, which was a debit card that we offered to college students. This was 1987, before credit cards were common for college kids. Parents would send us money, which we'd deposit in the student's account with us, and the students could then use their cards up to that amount. My role in the company was to convince every business in town to not only accept our card but to offer discounts to its users. At night, I also made deliveries from every restaurant that accepted our card. I was notoriously incapable of generating any tips, although one of my partners, Wende Biggs (daughter of Barton Biggs), always got great tips. And I had an unrequited crush on her. I'm glad she'll never read this; she won't, because she lives on a farm in France now.

What's wrong with college? First and foremost, it's too expensive. To send a kid to college you basically need up to $200,000. (I know the number is negotiable, but bear with me; I'm considering all expenses and a top-tier school.) That's insane. There's no way the incremental advantage your children get from having a diploma will ever pay that amount back. Perhaps for the first time ever, the opportunity cost ("opportunity cost" being a phrase I remember from Economics 101) of college does not equal the extra profits generated by the degree.

Then, too, I don't believe in a balanced education. Most colleges require kids to take a smattering of art, math, sciences, etc. Taking ten different courses a year on wildly different topics, with enormous homework responsibilities in each one, not to mention droning, boring professors for at least eight of the ten, is the surest formula for creating complete noninterest and inability to remember anything in any of the topics covered. What a waste of $200,000. There are far better uses of time.

What could a young person be doing instead of college? Working! Not just a labor or service job, either. There are many Internet-content jobs out there that are available to high school or college-age kids. I have high school and college kids working for me right now who are making more than $50,000 a year from writing gigs on the Internet. Kids can scour Craigslist for opportunities, beloved blogs, or Web sites related to their favorite interests. Companies are dying for good content. This is a good time to create one's own blog, get noticed, build relationships with other content companies and communities, and so on.

Why not take half the fee for one semester, give it to your kid, and tell him or her to start a revenue-generating business? Not everyone has entrepreneurial sensibilities, but it's always worth it to at least try once. And the cost for starting a business is next to zero, so it's a very viable alternative. What business should she start? For one thing, now that Facebook and MySpace have open development platforms, spec out a few applications for these platforms; for a few hundred dollars, outsource development of these applications to India, and get your friends to start trying them. Make sure they are viral (i.e., they should contain a message to "click here to get all your friends to try XYZ"), and see which ones are a success. I mention Facebook and MySpace because every kid is familiar with these sites and comfortable with the subtleties, and it's this comfort that can create the best businesses.

Youth is also a great time to spend a year trying to get good at one thing. Whatever your child's greatest interest now is, whether cooking, chess, writing, math, there are so many resources on the Internet available for learning that college is almost the last place a kid should go to pursue a passion. Intense, several-hour-a-day immersion in a favorite topic is the surest way to become an expert in that field.

Charity is another good alternative to college. Encourage your child to pick a favorite cause and do nothing but that for a semester or a year—build houses in Appalachia, for instance, or feed dinners to the homeless. Or you might take one semester's tuition, set up your own microcharity, and give the money out in $100 increments to good causes or situations your offspring thinks are worthy. Have him or her write up each situation in a notebook, and by the end, it will contain a whole life of lives changed.

And what about travel? Well, I'm not a big believer in that unless it's supervised. There's plenty of time to travel later in life. Right at home there's a plethora of opportunities that can far exceed the value of a college education at one-tenth the cost, and lead to greater experience and opportunities in career, wisdom, and life development.

It doesn't take detailed knowledge of string theory to appreciate a sunset. And *ka*, in addition to being a word that babies sometimes use, is also an ancient Egyptian word for a human soul. Don't try to make things overly complicated to fool people into thinking you're smart. Just make things as easy as possible, and learn from everything around you, not just the classroom.

26

Ask Not for Whom the Bell Tolls

I know you've felt it. That feeling of new love crystallizing over an initial coffee, a first date, a walk after a dinner, a conversation on a train. It's like a solar eclipse obscures the rest of your life. Everything else fades to black, and all you can do is stare at the halo of light surrounding the object of your affection. You want to look away, because everyone says you'll go blind. But you can't. You have to find out more. You have to know the answer to that very crucial question.

What question? Well, the one question that always comes up on a first date, of course: What power would you want to have if you were an evil supermutant? So let me put an end to all speculation on this question, go through all the possibilities, and inform you what the best one is. First off, it's not the obvious, reading minds. That's stupid. Look around you at people in the surrounding cubicles, across the dinner table, or at an executive committee meeting—you already know what they think of you. And if you don't, then being able to read their minds is not going to help much. Let me add that flying is out also. Where are you going to fly? People will see you and shoot you down. Super strength might be fun in a gym, but what are you going to do with it the rest of the time? Crush your desk? Lift your computer with one finger? Useless. And being able to live forever is going to come back and haunt you after the universe finishes its implosion into singularity and it's only you and your god left to chat for eternity.

Which brings us to the most important two: teleportation and time travel. I used to think teleportation was enough, because if I ever got hungry, I could always teleport into a McDonald's, grab a bunch of fries, and then teleport back out to the Yangtze River to finish my swim. In other words, money is meaningless to the teleporter. But ultimately, that ruins the fun of the chase. The pursuit of money *is* the end, not the means. Which leaves us only with time travel. And forget about the past. What you did on your summer vacation last year is of no interest to me. It's only the future, where all the possibilities are sewn together like disparate threads being woven into a single beautiful scarf. I want to know what that scarf looks like when it's done.

If you know even a single moment in the future, you can always use it to your advantage. But, not unlike the mind-reading power above, you *do* know the future. For instance, it's no secret that the sun will rise tomorrow. And that summer will occur again next year, no matter how desperately we hold on to this year's last vestiges now. We also know that everyone currently reading this book (and a few people who aren't) is going to eventually die.

The clock is ticking, my friends. More than 76 million Baby Boomers are preparing to retire right now. With retirement come the golden years in which they begin to cash in the chips they've accumulated and figure out how to enjoy the rest of their time. These might be very productive years, filled with joy they've never experienced. But when those years are over, there's only one possible ending. And it's right now that people begin to prepare for that eventuality.

The death industry is an oligopoly of sorts. Most people want to be buried in the ground, and there's only so much land that can accommodate them. So the companies that own the land and service it will win for a long time to come.

Let's look at Service Corp. International (SCI), which has 1,500 funeral homes and 400 cemeteries. It also just started a $200 million buyback program. This company, unlike most of us, clearly recognizes the future.

SERVICE CORPORATION INTERNATIONAL
as of Apr. 24, 2008

Splits: ▼

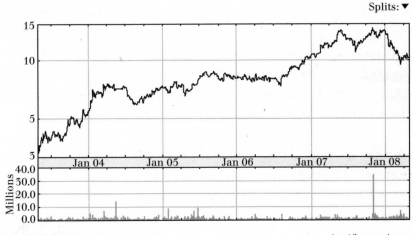

http://finance.yahoo.com

No less a prophet is Stewart Enterprises (STEI), which in 2007 bought back 7.7 million of its own shares. It has 223 funeral homes and 140 cemeteries.

STEWART ENTERPRISES, INC., CLASS A COMMON STOCK
as of Apr. 24, 2008

Splits: ▼

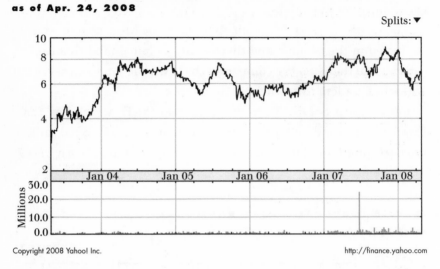

Copyright 2008 Yahoo! Inc.   http://finance.yahoo.com

With lumber prices increasing over the past five years, it's worth knowing where you can get a casket cheaply. Fear not. Costco (COST), a favorite of Warren Buffett sidekick and teenage wonder Charlie Munger, sells caskets wholesale.

COSTCO WHOLESALE
as of Apr. 24, 2008

Splits: ▼

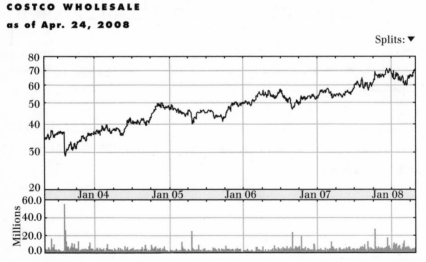

Copyright 2008 Yahoo! Inc.   http://finance.yahoo.com

And if you want to do away with caskets completely, Matthews Corporation (MATW) offers a full range of cremation products and services.

MATTHEWS INTERNATIONAL CORP.
as of Apr. 24, 2008

Splits: ▼

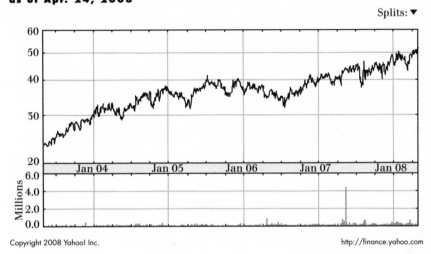

And finally, the granddaddy of the space, Hillenbrand (HB) offers the full gray spectrum from health-care products for the very elderly to caskets and cremation services.

When you really think about it, we all have amazing powers at our disposal. Perhaps foretelling the future would be the most powerful one to add.

27

Like Father, Like Son

In 1985, my dad made $5 million. Well, not really. He had a company, Consco Enterprises, which made accounting software for Fortune 100 companies. His company went public through a reverse merger, and on the day of the IPO his share of the illiquid stock was worth about $5 million. He never sold a share (the stock basically traded by appointment), and in 1989 the economy was not only going into an IT recession, but also mainframes (the platform his software worked on) were being rapidly replaced by PCs. The company quickly went bankrupt, or nearly bankrupt, and the assets were scooped up by Computer Associates for pennies on the dollar. My dad, frustrated and depressed over this turn of events, basically dropped out at this point and didn't work again, choosing to spend his days listening to music and thinking about what could've been.

When Consco first went public, he was riding high. He bought a house. He bought a car. He bought cars for all his employees. He rented a floor of the Plaza Hotel and threw a party. I remember someone telling me at the party that my dad was a genius. Another person told me they were going to buy the stock because you couldn't go wrong "betting on this guy" and pointed at my dad. Then, a few years later, when everything had gone down, he had trouble walking through a supermarket without breaking into tears. I went to visit once when things were at their lowest. "What's wrong with me?" he would say. "I feel like I'm in a permanent fog. When am I going to shake this off?" I was in college at the time, and my parents could no longer afford to put me through school. I ended up taking out loans, working forty hours a week at various odd jobs, and fortunately winning a chess tournament or two in order to pay tuition and eat three meals a day. (Well, I was hungry, so I would need four or five meals a day.)

A similar thing happened to me in the dot-com bust. I had made some money selling a Web services company in the heyday, and then I ended up losing a good chunk of it when everything fell to pieces. In 2001, in the depths of despair at having lost money, I tried everything: therapy, yoga, long walks, even meditation. I sat, Zen style, every day, and with a group three mornings a week. One time I went to an all-day sitting. Zen is a particularly painful form of meditation. The idea of the lotus position is to cut off circulation to your legs, forcing you to sit in sometimes excruciating pain but learn to deal with it (by being in the moment) so as to acquire the tools to deal with just about everything else in life. At one point in the all-day meditation, we all had to stand up to do a walking meditation. Everyone stood up, but I immediately fell over and couldn't move because my legs just simply had no feeling in them for a few minutes. The rest of the class walked around me.

All of this is to say: Nothing works. Tennyson's conclusion, 'Tis better to have loved and lost / Than never to have loved at all" is not true when it comes to money. (I'm not so sure it's true with love either.) Better to never have than to taste what feels like immortality and to have to part with it. I was able to learn from my mistakes and slowly climb out of the hole, becoming, I hope, a better person as a result. My dad's worries overcame him ultimately, and he passed away from a stroke two years ago.

One thing I learned in the process, as clichéd as it sounds, is that nothing is worth worrying about. As I write this, with the U.S. economy seemingly about to collapse, a run on the banks being discussed in the mainstream media, and the housing crisis on the verge of Depression-like proportions, it's easy to worry, or even to panic. But this, too, shall pass. And it's refreshing to see the greats loading up on the very financials and retailers that everyone is panicking away from. Buffett's buying up shares of Bank of America and Karmax. Lampert's buying shares in Citigroup (C) and even distressed retailer Restoration Hardware (RSTO). With persistence and diversification—both in your career and in your investments—and by learning to postpone worry for a brighter day, these moments of fear turn into long-term opportunities if taken advantage of. As for me, the Internet and investing have paid off for now. And I enjoy writing the occasional book. Unfortunately, my dad didn't live to see it.

28

Nothing Lasts Forever

I have an idea for a new TV channel. Bear with me for a second. I was in an airport terminal recently, and everyone was slack-jawed, staring blindly at the TV set. It was tuned to a news channel, and a woman who apparently had had some minor disagreement with a bartender was getting TASERed by a cop or security guard of some sort. He was following her all over the ground while she flailed about, screaming. The week before, I was in a restaurant that had a TV, and everyone was looking at a similar video, of a guy being TASERed because he disagreed with John Kerry in a very vocal manner. People love this stuff. There's something about watching a man, woman, or child being TASERed that really gets the adrenaline going. And for some reason, it seems that everyone who gets TASERed is also being videotaped. So let's get this going: the TASER Channel. People getting TASERed twenty-four hours a day. Maybe even make it a subscription channel—realistically, I don't think advertisers will like it that much.

The reason why I'm only half kidding is because a channel like this would in fact have millions of people watching it. It would be like Page 6 of the *New York Post*. Everyone would deny watching it, but secretly, at night, when they wake up from whatever insomnia plagues them in their dreams, they would creep downstairs, turn on channel 486, and watch America's Favorite TASER Channel until the sun rises.

It's sad, but humans like to watch, read, and spy on sorrow and pain. When the pain is being inflicted by another human, it's all the more fascinating. With our current media outlets, it's very hard to go on a "pain diet," i.e., avoid all exposure to the suffering around us. And why should we, you might ask, since suffering is reality. But hope is reality also. There is much suffering right now in the markets and the economy, and the pundits will be more than happy to tell you about it. Yes, there are people who have worked hard and own their first homes and are now going to lose them. Yes, with employment at a peak and a potential economic slowdown in certain sectors, many people will lose their jobs. Even 1 percent more unemployment means more than one million people will experience severe shortfalls in their quality of life. Despite any Fed cuts, banks have already stopped lending money, meaning that any hope for a fast resolution of these issues has been postponed for months, if not even a year or more. I was at a dinner recently made up of mostly investors, venture capitalists, bloggers, and the like, gathered to exchange ideas. Right in the middle of the entrée I heard a well-known pundit shout across his table, "The Fed is Wall Street's bitch," and everyone laughed at his colorful language as he went on to describe the disaster he foresaw.

But none of this is the way to make money. Staring slack-jawed at an economy that seems to be flailing on the ground ignores the fact that time and time again, the TASERed victims get up, walk around, and then appear on morning talk shows to tout the injustice they suffered (which allows us to repeatedly visit the videos under discussion). Look at twenty years ago, they tell us. The market was at all-time highs, then there was a surprise rate cut, a weakening dollar, followed by a crash. Look, because it's scary to imagine that it could happen again and we could watch a fall of 20 percent or more in the major indices.

But no, don't keep staring at that video. Every step of the way, buy hope and ignore the fear. Turn off the TV the next time someone is simply flailing and saying nothing of interest. Throughout this book I have tried (and, I hope, succeeded) to stick to the trends I believe will pay off, rather than engaging in cocktail-party discussion about what the Fed is doing wrong, how the United States is on the brink of collapse, or whatever it is people are talking about at parties—people rarely invite me to one. The essential themes are:

- **Focus on strong demographic trends** that will take shape throughout this next century, regardless of year-by-year or month-by-month economic conditions.
- **Follow in the footsteps of investors** who are far superior to us. They won't always be right, but it's a guarantee they've done more homework than we have, and if their choices also overlap with some of the trends I've mentioned, then it's a further indicator of a solid foundation.
- **Investment, career, and life decisions go hand in hand.** All of the demographic trends, and the style of thinking, described in this book can be applied to areas ranging from college to being an entrepreneur. Take advantage of the opportunities out there now, and don't wait for regrets to crop up.

PUZZLE ANSWERS

Across

4. Berkshire Hathaway
6. Bankrate
7. Howard Hughes
12. Disney
13. General Electric
14. D. E. Shaw
17. Bill Gates
18. The South Sea Company
19. George Soros
22. LevelThree
23. Autoliv
26. Cryptologic
30. Bank of New York
33. PetroChina
36. The *Washington Post*
38. Cohen
39. Luxottica
40. Berkowitz
41. Jerry Levin
42. Audible
44. Graham
45. Jupitermedia
46. Copart
47. America Online
49. Keynes
50. Symbolic
52. Carols Slim Helu
53. stagflation
54. Paulsen
55. tulip

Down

1. Franklin Resources
2. The Daily Journal Corporation
3. Mackay
5. Ken Fisher
8. American Express
9. Wesco
10. Jamba Juice
11. Phil Fisher
15. Procter and Gamble
16. Charlie Munger
18. The Hershey Company
20. Blackstone
21. Kerviel
24. Simons
25. J. P. Morgan
27. Salomon Brothers
28. David Dodd
29. Steve Case
31. Barton Biggs
32. Movil
34. Bank of America
35. Roosevelt
37. VeriSign
42. Amazon
43. Lycos
48. Omidyar
49. Kmart
51. Yahoo

INDEX

247